Picking the Lock of Time

Developing Chronology in American Archaeology

Edited by James Truncer

University Press of Florida

Gainesville / Tallahassee / Tampa / Boca Raton

Pensacola / Orlando / Miami / Jacksonville / Ft. Myers

08 07 06 05 04 03   6 5 4 3 2 1

Library of Congress Cataloging-in-Publication Data
Picking the lock of time: developing chronology in American archaeology / edited
by James Truncer.
p. cm.
Includes bibliographical references and index.
ISBN 0-8130-2678-4 (cloth: acid-free paper)
1. Archaeological dating—United States—History. 2. Indians of North America—
Antiquities. 3. United States—Antiquities. I. Truncer, James, 1959–.
CC78.P53 2003
973.1'1—dc21 2003054086

The University Press of Florida is the scholarly publishing agency for the State
University System of Florida, comprising Florida A&M University, Florida Atlantic
University, Florida Gulf Coast University, Florida International University, Florida
State University, University of Central Florida, University of Florida, University
of North Florida, University of South Florida, and University of West Florida.

University Press of Florida
15 Northwest 15th Street
Gainesville, FL 32611-2079
http://www.upf.com

Contents

Figures and Tables

Figures

Tables

Preface

To appreciate where archaeology is today, it is essential to know where it has been. Archaeologists are increasingly aware of the relevance of their discipline's history to understanding its present situation, as witnessed by a number of recent publications on the subject by both senior and junior scholars and the development of a history-of-archaeology interest group under the auspices of the Society for American Archaeology. Within the history of archaeology, perhaps no topic is more deserving of attention than the development of chronological method—the linchpin of archaeology.

Most of the chapters in this volume were originally papers presented in a symposium at the annual meeting of the Society for American Archaeology at Philadelphia in April 2000. I, for one, have found the enthusiasm of the participants infectious. I have greatly enjoyed my conversations with them and greatly benefited from their insights. I would like to thank all of the contributors and the editorial staff of the University Press of Florida, particularly Meredith Morris-Babb and John Byram, for their help and patience in bringing this project to fruition. I would also like to thank Andrew Christenson for indexing the book.

|

Introduction

James Truncer

Resolution of the "chronology problem" in the early twentieth century was one of the first real success stories of American archaeology. By formulating hypotheses that were empirically testable, it was possible, for the first time, to assess the age of archaeological phenomena in a way that retained the capacity to be wrong (Dunnell 1986b: 29). As a result, archaeology began to be viewed as a science by those outside the discipline—a change so remarkable that its practitioners considered themselves "new archaeologists" (Wissler 1917; Dunnell, this volume). This auspicious development paved the way for what has been termed the *culture history paradigm* in American prehistoric archaeology, which came to prominence roughly between 1910 and 1960 (Dunnell 1986a, 1986b; Lyman et al. 1997). Arguably, this was a productive, "normal science" period (Kuhn 1962) in which the principal interest of establishing spatial and temporal relations minimized other concerns such as object function (Dunnell 1986b: 29–30).

Culture history rested on the development and/or improvement and wider application of three methodological foundations: stratigraphy, seriation, and dendrochronology, the latter, as well as frequency seriation, being American contributions (e.g., Lyman et al. 1997: 53; Nash, this volume). All three methodologies figure prominently in the chapters of this book. The impact and utility of the chronometric methods developed during this period are, of course, still with us. As Lyman and O'Brien (2000b: 692) point out, the later invention of radiometric dating did not replace methods developed in the 1910s and 1920s; rather, the early chronometers "supplemented, and continue to supplement, the new chronometer."

Until lately, however, little attention has been paid to just how culture history developed, came to the fore, and fell into disfavor—attributable in part perhaps to the polemics of the second "new archaeology" after 1960.

Several recent comprehensive efforts document not only how the methods and techniques used in culture history worked but also why they worked—analyzing the underlying intellectual thought that made culture history possible (Lyman 2001; Lyman and O'Brien 1999, 2000a, 2000b; Lyman et al. 1997, 1998; O'Brien and Lyman 1998, 1999). These authors find that many of the cornerstones of culture history, such as using homologies and a materialist perspective to build historical lineages, are compatible with evolutionary theory. This approach has been criticized as "presentistic" and antithetical to modern practices that seek to understand historical developments "on their own terms" (Trigger 1998: 364). Dunnell (this volume) responds that since scientific disciplines are constantly in the process of overcoming and replacing commonsense propositions with theoretically justified ones, "to explain disciplinary development one must go beyond the 'facts' as seen by the participants and the explanations they erected." He argues, in other words, that the intellectual history of a science needs to be theoretically informed as well.

The spate of recent research concerning the intellectual history of culture history encourages a more detailed examination of other facets of its development. While the scientific mechanisms of culture history, once in place, operated independently of external influences such as social and political factors (indeed, this appears to be a hallmark of science; see Meltzer 1989: 17 and references therein), how did social and institutional contexts affect their development and application? What factors, in addition to intellectual concerns, guided the decisions of individuals involved in developing culture history? Addressing these questions will provide a fuller account of how culture history came about (Snead 2001, this volume).

While I agree with Trigger (1998: 366) regarding the need to "relate developments in archaeology to broader intellectual and social contexts," such efforts typically attempt to "discover" broad correlations between archaeological interpretation and the interests of governing social or economic groups (e.g., Patterson 1986; Trigger 1989: 14–15) or lean toward more deterministic relations between the two (e.g., Hinsley 1989; Kehoe 1989). One author has gone so far as to suggest that "nothing in archaeology can be considered strictly internal" (Hinsley 1989: 94). In developing a scientific approach to the chronology problem, however, American archaeology in the early decades of the twentieth century *did* establish a degree of autonomy that had not been enjoyed previously. For instance, the formulation of seriation, and the *chronological* conclusions able to be drawn from its application, *were* independent of social, political, and economic factors of the time. Any seriation can be evaluated empirically by anyone at anytime. Who applied it, as well as where and when it was applied, was much more susceptible to social and institutional influences, but these did not affect the results of the application. It was the post hoc cultural interpretations that were not theoretically warranted (for example, equating historical types and assemblages with "cultures"), as well as the lack of theory to explain why seriation worked, that proved to be the downfall of culture history (Dunnell 1986a, 1986b, this volume). Those identifying and criticizing the ethnocentric character of archaeological "interpretation" in general, as opposed to explanation (O'Brien 1996: 460–462), are quite right to do so, but the scientific approach to chronology in the early decades of the twentieth century provided one of the first glimpses of a viable alternative. While culture historians were ultimately not successful in replacing commonsense interpretations with theoretical explanations, their use of an empirical standard obviated a reliance on common sense to build chronology.

This volume focuses on the early contributors to cultural history—their achievements and failures as well as their pedagogical and institutional affiliations. All the major players are included: Andrew Douglass, William Holmes, Alfred Kidder, Alfred Kroeber, Nels Nelson, Frederic Putnam, Leslie Spier, and Clark Wissler. Less well known individuals, such as Dorothy Cross, Neil Judd, George Langford, and William Nickerson also shaped regional developments in culture history and are given some long-overdue attention. It is through examining the contributions and responses of individuals that the interaction between internal and external developments and their impact on the history of the discipline is most effectively assessed. As will become clear in these chapters, culture history did not proceed in a unified way; rather, it unfolded in fits and starts developmentally and regionally.

Both Dunnell and Nash point out that chronology was not an overriding concern of archaeologists at the turn of the twentieth century. Resolution of the "moundbuilder" controversy and the "American Paleolithic" question actually dampened interest in chronological issues (Dunnell, this volume). This does not mean that time was considered unimportant. Indeed, Holmes (1886a, 1886b) explicitly recognized chronology as a key issue early on. Tree-ring counting or averaging was not uncommon (Squier and Davis 1848: 16; Thomas 1894: 627–631; Wyman 1875: 83), and, as Browman (this volume) and O'Brien (this volume) show, stratigraphic excavation, no matter how defined or routinely performed, was conducted in the latter half of the nineteenth century. Browman (this volume) documents, in more detail than ever before, the pedagogical lineages of Americanist stratigraphic excavation and artifact recovery. The measurement or "marking" (as Nash puts it) of time was clearly of some interest to late-nineteenth- and early-twentieth-century archaeologists, even if it was not a dominant one.

A turning point in resolving the chronology problem appears not so much tied to development of technique (O'Brien, this volume; Snead, this volume) as to a change in the way variation is conceived—a change from an essentialist to a materialist ontology (Dunnell, this volume; O'Brien, this volume). As Dunnell (this volume) points out, once change was conceived as differences in amount (not kind) and quantified, a solution to the chronology problem quickly followed. Both Snead (this volume) and O'Brien (this volume) critically examine a defining moment in culture history: Nels Nelson's (1916) excavation at San Cristóbal, New Mexico, in November 1914. Snead provides a wealth of information on the institutional contexts that led to Nelson's important excavation, while O'Brien focuses on the intellectual significance of Nelson's insights. Together, these two chapters provide a fuller understanding of how Nelson's work at San Cristóbal was initiated and why it began to revolutionize American archaeology.

Leslie Spier's (1917a, 1917b) best-known contribution to early culture history is his stratigraphic test of Kroeber's initial work at Zuñi in 1916. Less well known is his attempt to use this Southwest experience to construct chronology from lithics recovered at Abbott Farm in New Jersey, a site that he, along with Alanson Skinner, helped excavate between 1914 and 1915 (Spier 1918). In hindsight, this attempt failed because his projectile point types mixed analogous and homologous attributes and because only coarse artifact-depth information was recorded for most of the excavated remains (Truncer, this volume). Unfortunately, Spier's innovative line of inquiry fell into a research vacuum in the 1920s. Research discontinuity is a theme that runs through several chapters in this volume (Browman, Christenson, Nash, and Truncer), the long-term deleterious effects of which often go unrecognized. Research discontinuity in archaeology is chronic, and such frequent disruption often means that commonsense explanatory frameworks are able to quietly replace scientific ones. This is precisely what happened in New Jersey when Dorothy Cross (1941) resumed work at Abbott Farm in the 1930s (Truncer, this volume).

Not so with George Langford (1927), an amateur archaeologist working in Illinois (Christenson, this volume), who, like William Nickerson (Browman, this volume), appears to have maintained and benefited from professional correspondence. Remarkably, Langford, working only on Sundays and holidays at the Fisher site near Joliet from 1924 to 1929, documented a stratigraphic time-depth that until then was not commonly recognized in the area. Along with Nickerson, Langford provided critical stratigraphic information to Fay-Cooper Cole and his University of Chicago students early in their archaeological survey of the state. Although still enmeshed in an essentialist metaphysic that identified differences in "cultures" rather than frequency change, Langford's excavations at the Fisher site contributed significantly to the development of midwestern archaeology. It is difficult to appreciate today the extent to which avocational archaeologists influenced the professionalization of the discipline in the first half of the twentieth century. George Langford, an amateur archaeologist who helped the University of Chicago archaeology program get started, is a prime example.

The debt owed professionals outside archaeology is demonstrated in Nash's (this volume) examination of Clark Wissler's corroboration with astronomer Andrew Douglass in the development of dendrochronology. Like Dunnell, Nash argues that chronology was not a pressing issue for most archaeologists at the beginning of the twentieth century. He goes on to suggest the reason for this indifference is that archaeologists at this time had backgrounds in the social sciences rather than the natural sciences. Why Cyrus Thomas, who recognized that the natural sciences could improve estimates of tree age (and therefore mound age) through measurements of average growth of tree species (Thomas 1894: 627–631), was apparently unaware of the late-eighteenth- and early-nineteenth-century crossdating works of von Burgsdorf, Twining, and Babbage remains a mystery. That interests in chronology and the natural sciences are linked appears to hold some merit, since W. H. Holmes, another late-nineteenth-century archaeologist with an appreciation of the natural sciences, was one of only a few at that time to identify chronology as a priority (Holmes 1886a, 1886b).

How the chronological problem was solved in the early twentieth century is germane today because early culture historians first succeeded in what continues to be a long-term goal for most archaeologists: making archaeology scientific. In doing so, culture historians developed *archaeological* methods that remain central to the discipline. Challenged with the knotty problem of chronology, how *did* early culture historians go about solving it? What can we learn from their solution? In contemplating the intellectual developments, as well as the institutional and social contexts associated with resolving chronology, one cannot help but think of similarly unresolved issues in contemporary archaeology and what will be required to overcome them. In studying the history of archaeology, we are reminded that we are not the first in the field to confront thorny issues or apparent impasses. Viewed in this light, the giant success of the first "new archaeologists" is not only reassuring but also instructive. The answers to some of our current dilemmas may lie, as it did for early culture historians, in making our propositions susceptible to empirical falsification and analyzing change using a materialist ontology. With the benefit of hindsight, we can identify (and hopefully address) some recurrent problems in conducting archaeological research (for example, research discontinuity and inadequate analytical units). It is this cumulative quality that distinguishes the history of a science; as Meltzer (1989: 11) puts it, "What we know today builds upon, is constrained by, or is in reaction to past knowledge." In this sense, we are still learning from early culture historians, not only from their successes and limitations but also from the contexts and processes that framed their construction of the first new archaeology.

References

Cross, D. 1941. *Archaeology of New Jersey.* Vol. 1. Trenton: Archaeological Society of New Jersey and the New Jersey State Museum.

Dunnell, R. C. 1986a. "Methodological Issues in Americanist Artifact Classification." In *Advances in Archaeological Method and Theory,* vol. 9, edited by M. B. Schiffer, 149–207. New York: Academic Press.

———. 1986b. "Five Decades of American Archaeology." In *American Archaeology: Past and Future,* edited by D. J. Meltzer, D. D. Fowler, and J. A. Sabloff, 23–49. Washington, D.C.: Smithsonian Institution Press.

Hinsley, C. M. 1989. "Revising and Revisioning the History of Archaeology: Reflections on Region and Context." In *Tracing Archaeology's Past: The Historiography of Archaeology,* edited by A. L. Christenson, 79–96. Carbondale: Southern Illinois University Press.

Holmes, W. H. 1886a. "Pottery of the Ancient Pueblos." *Fourth Annual Report of the Bureau of Ethnology, 1882–83,* 257–360. Washington, D.C.: Government Printing Office.

———. 1886b. "Ancient Pottery of the Mississippi Valley." *Fourth Annual Report of the Bureau of Ethnology, 1882–83,* 361–436. Washington, D.C.: Government Printing Office.

Kehoe, A. B. 1989. "Contexualizing Archaeology." In *Tracing Archaeology's Past: The Historiography of Archaeology,* edited by A. L. Christenson, 97–106. Carbondale: Southern Illinois University Press.

Kroeber, A. L. 1916a. "Zuñi Culture Sequences." *National Academy of Sciences, Proceedings* 2: 42–45.

———. 1916b. "Zuñi Potsherds." *American Museum of Natural History, Anthropological Papers* 18 (1): 1–37.

Kuhn, T. S. 1962. *The Structure of Scientific Revolutions.* Chicago: University of Chicago Press.

Langford, G. 1927. "The Fisher Mound Group, Successive Aboriginal Occupations Near the Mouth of the Illinois River." *American Anthropologist* 29: 153–205.

Lyman, R. L. 2001. "Culture Historical and Biological Approaches to Identifying Homologous Traits." In *Style and Function: Conceptual Issues in Evolutionary Archaeology,* edited by T. D. Hurt and G. F. M. Rakita, 69–89. Westport, Conn.: Bergin and Garvey Press.

Lyman, R. L., and M. J. O'Brien. 1999. "Americanist Stratigraphic Excavation and the Measurement of Culture Change." *Journal of Archaeological Method and Theory* 6: 55–108.

———. 2000a. "Measuring and Explaining Change in Artifact Variation with Clade-Diversity Diagrams." *Journal of Anthropological Archaeology* 19: 39–74.

———. 2000b. "Chronometers and Units in Early Archaeology and Paleontology." *American Antiquity* 65: 691–707.

Lyman, R. L., M. J. O'Brien, and R. C. Dunnell. 1997. *The Rise and Fall of Culture History.* New York: Plenum Press.

Lyman, R. L., S. Wolverton, and M. J. O'Brien. 1998. "Seriation, Superposition, and Interdigitation: A History of Americanist Graphic Depictions of Culture Change." *American Antiquity* 63: 239–261.

Meltzer, D. J. 1989. "A Question of Relevance." In *Tracing Archaeology's Past: The Historiography of Archaeology,* edited by A. L. Christenson, 5–19. Carbondale: Southern Illinois University Press.

Nelson, N. C. 1916. "Chronology of the Tano Ruins, New Mexico." *American Anthropologist* 18: 159–180.

O'Brien, M. J. 1996. *Paradigms of the Past: The Story of Missouri Archaeology.* Columbia: University of Missouri Press.

O'Brien, M. J., and R. L. Lyman. 1998. *James A. Ford and the Growth of Americanist Archaeology.* Columbia: University of Missouri Press.

———. 1999. *Seriation, Stratigraphy, and Index Fossils: The Backbone of Archaeological Dating.* New York: Kluwer Academic/Plenum Press.

Patterson, T. C. 1986. "The Last Sixty Years: Toward a Social History of Americanist Archaeology in the United States." *American Anthropologist* 88: 7–26.

Snead, J. E. 2001. *Ruins and Rivals: The Making of Southwest Archaeology.* Tucson: University of Arizona Press.

Spier, L. 1917a. "An Outline for a Chronology of Zuñi Ruins." *American Museum of Natural History, Anthropological Papers* 18 (3): 207–331.

————. 1917b. "Zuñi Chronology." *National Academy of Sciences, Proceedings* 3: 280–283.

————. 1918. "The Trenton Argillite Culture." *American Museum of Natural History, Anthropological Papers* 22 (4): 167–226.

Squier, E. G., and E. H. Davis. 1848. *Ancient Monuments of the Mississippi Valley.* Smithsonian Contributions to Knowledge 1. Washington, D.C.

Thomas, C. 1894. "Report on the Mound Explorations of the Bureau of Ethnology." *Twelfth Annual Report of the Bureau of Ethnology, 1890–91,* 3–742. Washington, D.C.: Government Printing Office.

Trigger, B. G. 1989. *A History of Archaeological Thought.* Cambridge: Cambridge University Press.

————. 1998. Review of *The Rise and Fall of Culture History,* by R. L. Lyman, M. J. O'Brien, and R. C. Dunnell. *Journal of Field Archaeology* 25: 363–366.

Wissler, C. 1917. "The New Archaeology." *American Museum Journal* 17: 100–101.

Wyman, J. 1875. "Fresh-Water Shell Mounds of the St. John's River, Florida." *Peabody Academy of Science, Memoir* 4. Salem, Mass.

2

The First New Archaeology and the Development of Chronological Method

Robert C. Dunnell

History is not just a string of events, the factual nature of which is self-evident. Facts are not "discovered"; facts are created. They result from the interaction of phenomena and the mental tools for their description and explanation. In scientific disciplines, these tools are called *theory*. When facts are treated as discoveries, it is ego's own cultural background that takes the place of theory, and when the "facts" are commonsensical, so are the explanations. The history of scientific disciplines is necessarily one of overcoming and replacing commonsense questions, descriptions, and explanations with theoretically justified ones (e.g., Mierzecki 1991; Panchen 1992). Consequently, to explain disciplinary development, one must go beyond the "facts" as seen by the participants and the explanations they erected for them.

In recent archaeological literature, the term *new archaeology* is more or less synonymous with the so-called processual school (e.g., Caldwell 1959; Flannery 1967) of midcentury. It is easy to forget that early-twentieth-century archaeologists also thought of themselves as "new archaeologists" (for example, Wissler 1917), arguably with far better justification. Elsewhere (Dunnell 1986) I have argued that this revolution, which has since come to be known as *culture history*, was the first real paradigm in archaeology and that it was predicated on the development of chronological method, in particular, seriation, which was at once distinctly archaeological in nature, generally applicable, and delivered empirically testable results.

Background

In the nineteenth century, chronology was not the be-all, end-all of the emerging field of archaeology. Vying for attention were function, spatial patterning, technology, and the ever-persistent psychocultural "meaning" of archaeological materials, to name only the most obvious competitors (e.g., Evans 1872; Lubbock 1870; Squier and Davis 1848; Thomas 1894). The driving force behind archaeological work throughout most of the nineteenth century was simply discovery. Only a tiny fraction of what we now regard as the archaeological record was known. Some phenomena had not yet attracted notice; other phenomena were not appreciated as the handiwork of people. Not surprisingly, the archaeological record was described initially in commonsensical terms, that is, English words assigned by analogy with familiar devices of our own or other cultures. As a consequence, archaeological understandings in vogue at that time involved processes believed to explain everyday occurrences.[1]

In retrospect, one factor dominated change in archaeological practice and set the stage for radical change at the end of the nineteenth century: the desire to make archaeology science (e.g., Squier and Davis 1848; Holmes 1886a, 1892; see also Dunnell 1992 for a more in-depth analysis of this issue). There can be little doubt that asserting that archaeology was, or should be, a science began to legitimize activities and ideas otherwise without obvious warrant. Indeed, the assertion continues to be used in that manner today in many fields, including archaeology (as in CRM-enabling legislation). Regardless, once this rationalization was generally accepted in the late nineteenth century, becoming scientific became a serious motivating force in the field (e.g., Holmes 1892) and set the stage for the developments of interest in this volume.

The notion of science held by nineteenth-century archaeologists is inappropriate by modern standards, however, and did not favor the development of chronology. People like William Henry Holmes clearly embraced a physics model of science most of the time (Meltzer and Dunnell 1992).[2] This entails an essentialist view of reality (shared with Western common sense), treats time as an elapsed quantity (rather than age), and explains using laws that relate interactions among the fixed, repetitive entities (essences) thereby created. It is a model that continues to plague most archaeology, and it is a primary reason for our failure to reach our scientific objectives (Dunnell 1982). In sciences that employ an essentialist ontology, the key feature of relevance is their ahistoric nature. They conceive phenomena without past or future; this is how the "hard sciences" are able to "predict."[3] The impact of this view of reality on the development of chronologic method has been enormous. Perhaps the most deleterious element is the conception of time as a series of boxes (today called *phases*); precision is improved by subdivision into finer boxes. The parallel with Ptolemic epicircles is too striking to ignore. What made this approach anachronistic even in the late nineteenth century was the availability of a materialist model of science, Darwinian evolution, that explains change (rather than difference) and is thus far more appropriate to a scientific archaeology. Ironically, Holmes abandons his physics view of science in favor of contemporary evolutionary theory (ontogeny recapitulates the phylogeny of Haeckel [1877]) in his one great scientific triumph, the destruction of the "American Paleolithic" (Meltzer and Dunnell 1992).

The emergence of "problems," particularly two great problems of broad interest—the questions of the "moundbuilders" and of "early man"—during the second half of the nineteenth century, marks a shift away from simple ad hoc discovery (Phillips 1973). These were, however, commonsense questions that were stimulated directly by public interest rather than by internal professional concern. Both preceded the emergence of anything that might be called archaeological theory, and each assumed little beyond artifacts as manmade objects/places and the crudest of formal comparisons. While we certainly see these questions as having a strong chronological component today, it was not so obvious then, and, in the absence of archaeological theory, efforts to answer them were largely nonchronological.

The moundbuilder question was a nonproblem almost from the start. America's first great scientist, Samuel Morton, had demonstrated that the remains of the people interred in aboriginal mounds differed in no respect from known Amerindian crania (Morton 1839). Indeed, had it not been for the revival of the idea of moundbuilders as a distinct race by Squier and Davis (1848), one suspects the notion would have passed completely from learned circles by midcentury. The Smithsonian Institution was the undisputed leader in archaeological research in the nineteenth century (Sabloff and Willey 1980; Trigger 1989), and debunking the moundbuilder as a separate race became a major theme of its work for much of the rest of the century. John Wesley Powell, director of the Smithsonian's Bureau of Ethnology from its inception, treated the Indian origin of mounds as axiomatic. Thus Thomas's (1894) treatise on eastern mounds, far from being the ground-breaking study of this matter as sometimes depicted (for example, Sabloff and Willey 1980), was rather the last time it would occupy the professional literature in a major way. This resolution, however, led away from chronology. In positing two peoples, one replacing the other, the moundbuilder thesis had simple but unavoidable temporal implications. The Indian as moundbuilder diminished the importance of even that crude sense of time.

If the moundbuilder debate was mostly a lay controversy, professionals nearly came to blows on the antiquity of the occupation of the New World. Initially interest focused on the age of occupation independently of "who" those occupants might have been. On the one hand, the "Eolith" hypothesis relied heavily upon selection of a few rocks that resembled primitive tools from many that did not in geologic deposits. This often led to claims of great antiquity (see Grayson 1986 and references therein). Central was the definition of artifact itself, and, while the initial claims of great antiquity were relinquished by the early years of the twentieth century, less grandiose controversy of this kind persists to the present. The persistent lack of theory, which could have rephrased the question in a solvable form, is a likely culprit. Instead of seeking to identify the *agents* of physical processes, those who participate in this debate typically assert that there are one or more physical attributes that uniquely signify the work of *Homo* (for example, spiral fractures of bone).

Other efforts (e.g., Abbott 1876, 1881; Putnam 1889) identified artifacts analogous to, if not identical with, well-established European Paleolithic cultural units. The identification of a Paleolithic in North America would argue for a Pleistocene human presence here (Meltzer and Dunnell 1992). Although the artificial character of the objects in question was not contended, the issue was still one of how the archaeological record should be described—typology. This matter was effectively laid to rest by Holmes (1892), ironically by using evolutionary theory to show that proponents of the American Paleolithic (Meltzer and Dunnell 1992) had routinely mistaken unfinished artifacts for primitive finished artifacts. Holmes's analogy was incorrectly drawn from a modern point of view but was devastatingly effective at the time. Once again, however, by explaining variation as technological rather than chronological, the effect was to make chronological control less important in understanding American antiquities.

Essentialism and Materialism

Far from being a philosophical nicety, the distinction between materialism and essentialism, to which allusion has been made, is critical to understanding the development of chronological methods in archaeology. In essentialism, the phenomenological world is seen as being constituted by a large number of empirical kinds. The interactions between such units can therefore be accounted for by a set of laws. There are two critical methodological imperatives that follow. First, since kinds are "real," a central analytic effort of essentialist science is to *discover* "real" units, an inductive effort. Difference must be sorted from noise. Those operating within this framework treat archaeological types as "real." Quantification, when employed (and it need not be), is used to generate qualities or kinds by assessing the "significance" of variation (see also Luedtke 1986). Analysis is thus a matter of discovering discontinuities, "joints," as a famous archaeologist once termed it; kind itself becomes explanatory.

In materialism, the phenomenological world is seen as in the process of becoming; kinds, units, are analytic constructions imposed on reality. Because there are no fixed entities, there can be no fixed relations among them, that is, there can be no laws in a Newtonian sense. Types are not real (that is, one cannot appeal to their "reality" or "existence" in justification) but are simply templates that allow us to measure variability in amount. This position gives rise to the notion of change (temporal dimension) in addition to difference (spatial dimension).[4] Variation, not essence or kind, is the methodological target. Analysis produces continuity. Consequently, quantification is required. Explanation is a history of the conditions that determine the operation of laws. The relation between materialist and essentialist science, therefore, is also hierarchic; materialistic sciences always contain one or more essentialist sciences at a lower level in their structure. Thus Popper's (1957) famous dictum that there are no laws of history but the unfolding of history is governed by laws.

Without belaboring these distinctions, it should be easy to see why the first sciences were essentialist and why the model of science adopted initially by archaeologists would also be essentialist. Essentialism is the structure of common sense. It should be just as easy to appreciate that development of chronological methods if archaeology was constrained by this mind-set. Two things had to occur: (1) commonsense units, "real" types, had to be replaced by theoretical, or analytic ones, and (2) archaeological materials had to be quantified using such units.

Development of a Chronologic Method

In the case of archaeology, there was no a priori theory that could be employed to generate analytic units in the late nineteenth or early twentieth centuries. Consequently, an empiricist, trial-and-error tack was followed, and it left a large component of development to chance. In practical terms it meant that artifacts of known ages had to be described in various ways until an approach to description led to characterizations that consistently correlated with age. Once such units were in hand, their quantification led directly to seriation, the key chronological method, albeit still in a theoretical vacuum because of its ad hoc origin.

As noted, early description simply used English. By the late nineteenth century, attempts were being made to construct observational meta-languages, but the absence of any archaeological theory is clearly manifest. Charles Rau (1876) and Thomas Wilson (1889, 1899) began this effort by considering pointed bifaces (Dunnell 1986). This might seem like a strange starting point, inasmuch as ceramics are the typical modern typological target. Intuitively (that is, using common sense), however, whole objects were required to construct a classification. A substantial corpus of whole lithics was in research hands earlier than whole pots. Remarkably, the Rau-Wilson classification is explicit on the choice of criteria used to describe points—they were geometric parameters of shape (reinforcing the importance of "whole" objects). It aspired to no higher goal than to facilitate communication and reduce the words necessary to describe large series of objects (still cited by some as the rationale for classification). Nonetheless, Rau and Wilson were clearly disappointed that no spatial, temporal, or functional (not circular) structure could be observed as a result (Dunnell 1986).

Later, Holmes (1886b), working with pottery, appreciated that the solution to archaeological chronology lay in artifact variability; he went so far as to discount the use of pot shape as a relevant criterion for description because it was most likely functional (was he implying that he had other goals, temporal, spatial, ethnic?) (Holmes 1886c). But once again, the lack of any theory that could have generated relevant criteria led him to mix time with space and vice versa, even in his magnum opus on eastern ceramics (Holmes 1903). His major ceramic groups are ahistoric and only of passing historical interest today. In fact, he relied heavily upon the work of Clarence B. Moore, an amateur, for much of the chronology evident in the volume.

Later still, Max Uhle (1907) suggested that variations could be linked to time through stratigraphy, but his suggestion was criticized by Kroeber (1909), who attributed such difference to statistical noise or minor ethnic differences. Some, like Fowke (1896), took all such variation as meaningless noise—the product of "savage mechanics." For all this thrashing about, the issue of the "reality" of types never really comes up. Archaeologists *knew* they were not real because they were actively manipulating the terms of descriptions. The claim that types were real came up only in the later effort to synthesize and justify the types that had been developed by trial and error (Krieger 1944; Rouse 1939; see Dunnell 1986). This would produce untold mischief later on (e.g., Ford 1954; Read 1974; Spaulding 1953; Whallon 1972).

The first and most ingenious solution was invented by A. L. Kroeber (1916).[5] It was ingenious because he used contemporary observations about age to erect a chronology of southwestern settlements: state of occupancy (occupied/not occupied, but remembered as a place of former occupation/and not remembered) and a simple assumption that preservation was grossly and inversely correlated with age. Then he characterized ceramics from those locations so that some kinds typified the modern settlements while others dominated the prehistoric ones. Because the pottery sherds comprising each collection were not assignable to a single class using this approach, his tack was inherently quantitative. Realizing the weakness of his chronological yardstick and the lack of a theoretical warrant that posed problems for credibility, he recommended an empirical approach using stratigraphy (an established, nonarchaeological method) to test seriation results. This historical accident, forgivable in the developmental stages of a science, thwarted theoretical development for decades to come (Dunnell 1986).

Stratigraphy, superposition in particular, was well established in geology as a means of assigning ordinal ages to sedimentary deposits. Stratigraphy had also been a key tool in the development of European archaeology, and Americans still took their intellectual leads from Europeans. The "fact" of stratigraphy had been appreciated by Americans from the eighteenth century on, notably by Jefferson (1801) (see also Brackinridge 1814, Moore 1892, and Wyman 1875 for clear examples). Apart from the suggestion that there were prepottery and pottery horizons, however, the simple observation and recording of stratigraphic superposition did not lead to robust chronological tools. The reasons for this are clear in retrospect. First, ad hoc (commonsense) descriptions using English terms tend to be strongly functional. If the record were described in such terms, only the grossest kinds of change (like pottery/prepottery) would not be overwhelmed by nonchronological variation. Second, until the composition of stratigraphic units was described quantitatively, there appeared to be no chronological correlates of any descriptions. N. C. Nelson, whose understanding of stratigraphy was the most sophisticated in North America (for example, Nelson 1916, 1917, 1918), played a critical role (O'Brien and

Lyman 1999). Even though he drew explicitly upon the European strati-graphic model and realized the central role that superposition had to play in chronology, his essentialist underpinnings led him to expect differences in kind, not differences in amount. Once quantification, even relatively crude quantification, was employed with stylistic types, however, workers everywhere quickly solved the chronological problem. Thus Spier (1917) was able to test Kroeber's method at Zuñi ruins only one year following Kroeber's proposal. Lest the importance of using a stylistic description be forgotten, as Nelson (1916) foresaw, Spier (1916, 1918) and Wissler's (1916) efforts to employ similar methods in New Jersey failed, at least in part, because their descriptions were largely functional (see Truncer, this volume). Indeed, this is generally a problem with stone tools, contrary to modern practice (contra, for example, Close 1978, Sackett 1985); techno-logical and functional constraints virtually guarantee that truly neutral variation is usually minimal.

Ironically, although almost all of the key developments took place first in the American Southwest, seriation never came to play the crucial role in the construction of chronologies there that it did elsewhere. Sherd count-ing continued, to be sure, but the availability of dendrochronological dat-ing in this region led to the construction of stylistic types of short duration. Such types are well adapted to the essentialist index fossil approach (O'Brien and Lyman 1999) but anathema to quantification (Dunnell 1970).

Because American archaeologists backed into seriation, the reasons for the success of chronological ordering remained obscure until relatively recent time (Dunnell 1982). One consequence was that the number of archaeologists who actually built chronologies is rather limited. Most ar-chaeologists were users of chronologies built by others, and this use al-most always resorts to the use of essentialist constructions like phases. Also, even after radiocarbon dating confirmed the accuracy of seriation, many, if not most, archaeologists ignored it as a tool simply because it was not intuitively clear why it should work. For the same reasons, stratigra-phy was accorded an importance that it really did not warrant, even by many committed to seriation (e.g., Ford in Phillips et al. 1951; see also O'Brien and Lyman 1999). Only in the last few years has some of the potential of the breakthroughs of the first new archaeology come to be realized (Lipo et al. 1997; Neiman 1995).

Conclusions

The uniqueness of archaeology as a field of endeavor, its claim to science, even its public persona are intimately tied to its interest in and dependence on chronology and those constructs (like history, development, evolution) that chronology makes possible. It should not be surprising to see that the first methodological consensus, the first paradigm if you will—culture history—developed around the tools to construct archaeological chronologies. What is more interesting is the way in which archaeology seemed to back into the solution of its most difficult problem. Trial and error and accident dominated, not flashing intellectual insight. As a result, and in spite of the fact that American archaeology, using general methods to solve general problems, could be said to have produced empirically testable results from the second decade of the century on, archaeology never really became a science in its own right. The failure to replace ad hoc, commonsense rationalization with explicit theory lies at the heart of this larger failure and, as some clearly feel today, disillusionment with scientific goal itself. What is most ironic is that in the rush to be empirical, the sine qua non of science, practitioners omitted ontological and methodological inquiry that would have led to explicit rationalization of their methods and opened the door to systematic development.

Notes

1. Thus uniformitarism (Lyell 1837) is not the great methodological leap forward it is often made out to be; alternatively, it is easy to appreciate why such a concept should have been an early stepping-stone to a science of history.

2. If the frequent citation of Holmes to the exclusion of other contemporary archaeologists is puzzling, it is because Holmes—uniquely for the era—pursued a "philosophic approach" (Mason 1886), *methodologizing* in today's parlance (Embree 1992).

3. Prediction, in the sense of forecasting future outcomes, is often taken as distinguishing science from other explanatory systems. This is an illusion of essentialist science created by its merging of past and future into a single unchanging universe of laws. By substituting "time" in place of "age" (see Morris 1984 for a fuller account), the "why" questions of materialist science are reduced to "how" questions (for example, Mayr 1959, 1976).

4. Archaeologists routinely conflate change and difference as the meanings are intended here. By calling differences (in kind) of different ages "change," continuity is implied where none exists. That the terms are used as synonyms is revealed by the oft-encountered phrase "change in time." Déjà vu all over again!

5. Sir Flinders Petrie is usually given credit for the invention of seriation, and while his "Sequences in Prehistoric Remains" (1899) clearly is an example of the method, there is nothing to suggest that Kroeber was aware of this paper or that he borrowed from it, inasmuch as the two take different approaches to the problem.

References

Abbott, C. C. 1876. "The Stone Age in New Jersey." *Annual Report of the Smithsonian Institution for 1875*, 246–389. Washington, D.C.: U.S. Government Printing Office.

———. 1881. *Primitive Industry*. Salem, Mass.: George Bates.

Brackenridge, H. M. 1814. *Views of Louisiana; Together with a Journal of a Voyage Up the Missouri River in 1811*. Pittsburgh: Cramer, Spear and Eichblam.

Caldwell, J. R. 1959. "The New American Archaeology." *Science* 129: 303–307.

Close, A. 1978. "The Identification of Style in Lithic Artifacts." *World Archaeology* 10: 223–237.

Dunnell, R. C. 1970. "Seriation Method and Its Evaluation." *American Antiquity* 35: 305–319.

———. 1982. "Science, Social Science, and Common Sense: The Agonizing Dilemma of Modern Archaeology." *Journal of Anthropological Research* 38: 1–25.

———. 1986. "Methodological Issues in Americanist Artifact Classification." In *Advances in Archaeological Method and Theory*, vol. 9, edited by M. B. Schiffer, 149–207. New York: Academic Press.

———. 1992. "Is a Scientific Archaeology Possible?" In Embree, *Metaarchaeology*, 75–97.

Embree, L., ed. 1992. *Metaarchaeology*. Dordrecht, Netherlands: Kluwer Press.

Evans, J. 1872. *The Ancient Stone Implements, Weapons, and Ornaments of Great Britain*. New York: D. Appleton.

Flannery, K. V. 1967. Review of *An Introduction to American Archaeology*, vol. 1 of *North and Middle America*, by G. R. Willey. *Scientific American* 217 (2): 119–122.

Ford, J. A. 1954. "Comment on A. C. Spaulding's `Statistical Techniques for the Discovery of Artifact Types.'" *American Antiquity* 19: 390–391.

Fowke, G. 1896. "Stone Art." *Thirteenth Annual Report, Bureau of American Ethnology*, 57–178. Washington, D.C.: U.S. Government Printing Office.

Grayson, D. K. 1986. "Eoliths, Archaeological Ambiguity, and the Generation of 'Middle Range' Research." In *American Archaeology: Past and Future*, edited by D. J. Meltzer, D. D. Fowler, and J. A. Sabloff, 77–133. Washington, D.C.: Smithsonian Institution Press.

Haeckel, E. 1877. *Anthropogenie oder Entwickelungeschicte des Menschen* [Anthropogenesis or developmental history of humans]. 3rd ed. Leipzig: Engelman.

Holmes, W. H. 1886a. "Origin and Development of Form and Ornamentation in Ceramic Art." *Fourth Annual Report of the Bureau of Ethnology, 1882–83,* 437–465. Washington, D.C.: Government Printing Office.

———. 1886b. "Ancient Pottery of the Mississippi Valley." *Fourth Annual Report of the Bureau of Ethnology, 1882–83,* 361–436. Washington, D.C.: U.S. Government Printing Office.

———. 1886c. "Pottery of the Ancient Pueblos." *Fourth Annual Report of the Bureau of Ethnology, 1882–83,* 257–360. Washington, D.C.: U.S. Government Printing Office.

———. 1892. "Evolution of the Aesthetic." *Proceedings, Forty-First Meeting of the Association for the Advancement of Science, Rochester, 1892,* 239–255.

———. 1903. "Aboriginal Pottery of the Eastern United States." *Twentieth Annual Report of the Bureau of American Ethnology, 1898–99,* 1–201. Washington, D.C.: U.S. Government Printing Office.

Jefferson, T. 1801. *Notes on the State of Virginia.* New York: Furman and Loudan.

Krieger, A. D. 1944. "The Typological Concept." *American Antiquity* 9: 271–288.

Kroeber, A. L. 1909. "The Archaeology of California." In *Putnam Anniversary Volume,* edited by F. Boas, 1–42. New York: Stechert.

———. 1916. "Zuñi Potsherds." *American Museum of Natural History, Anthropological Papers* 18 (1): 1–37.

Lipo, C., M. Madsen, R. C. Dunnell, and T. Hunt 1997. "Population Structure, Cultural Transmission, and Frequency Seriation." *Journal of Anthropological Archaeology* 16: 301–333.

Lubbock, J. 1870. *The Origin of Civilisation and the Primitive Condition of Man.* London: Williams and Norgate.

Luedtke, B. E. 1986. "Flexible Tools for Constructing the Past." *Man in the Northeast* 31: 89–98.

Lyell, C. 1837. *Principles of Geology; Being an Inquiry into How Far the Former Changes in the Earth's Surface Are Referable to Causes Now in Operation.* 4 vols. 5th ed. London: John Murray.

Mason, O. T. 1886. "Anthropology." *Annual Report of the Smithsonian Institution for 1885,* 815–817. Washington, D.C.: U.S. Government Printing Office.

Mayr, E. 1959. "Typological versus Population Thinking." In *Evolution and Anthropology: A Centennial Appraisal,* edited by B. J. Meggers, 409–412. Washington, D.C.: The Anthropological Society of Washington.

———. 1976. *Evolution and the Diversity of Life.* Cambridge: Harvard University Press.

Meltzer, D. J., and R. C. Dunnell, eds. 1992. *The Archaeology of William Henry Holmes.* Editors' Introduction, vii–l. Washington, D.C.: Smithsonian Institution Press.

Mierzecki, R. 1991. *The Historical Development of Chemical Concepts.* Dordrecht, Netherlands: Kluwer Press.

Moore, C. B. 1892. "Certain Shell Heaps of the St. John's River, Florida, Hitherto Unexplored." *American Naturalist* 26: 912–922.

Morris, R. 1984. *Time's Arrow: Scientific Attitudes Toward Time.* New York: Simon and Schuster.

Morton, S. G. 1839. *Crania Americana; or a Comparative View of the Skulls of Various Aboriginal Nations of North and South America.* Philadelphia: J. Dobson.

Neiman, F. D. 1995. "Stylistic Variation in Evolutionary Perspective: Inferences from Decorative Diversity and Interassemblage Distance in Illinois Woodland Ceramic Assemblages." *American Antiquity* 60: 7–36.

Nelson, N. C. 1916. "Chronology of the Tano Ruins, New Mexico." *American Anthropologist* 18: 159–180.

———. 1917. "Contributions to the Archaeology of Mammoth Cave and Vicinity, Kentucky." *American Museum of Natural History, Anthropological Papers* 22 (1): 1–74.

———. 1918. "Chronology in Florida." *American Museum of Natural History, Anthropological Papers* 22 (2): 74–103.

O'Brien, M. J., and R. L. Lyman. 1999. *Seriation, Stratigraphy, and Index Fossils.* New York: Plenum.

Panchen, A. L. 1992. *Classification, Evolution, and the Nature of Biology.* Cambridge: Cambridge University Press.

Petrie, Sir W.M.F. 1899. "Sequences in Prehistoric Remains." *Journal of the Royal Anthropological Institute of Great Britain and Ireland* 29: 295–301.

Phillips, P. 1973. Introduction to *The Archaeological Reports of Frederick Ward Putnam,* ix–xii. In *Antiquities of the New World,* vol. 8. Cambridge: Harvard University Press.

Phillips, P., J. A. Ford, and J. B. Griffin. 1951. *Archaeological Survey in the Lower Mississippi Valley, 1940–1947.* Peabody Museum of American Archaeology and Ethnology, Papers 25. Cambridge, Mass.

Popper, K. 1957. *The Poverty of Historicism.* New York: Basic Books.

Putnam, F. W. 1889. Discussion, "The Aborigines of the District of Columbia and the Lower Potomac." *American Anthropologist* 2: 241–246.

Rau, C. 1876. *The Archaeological Collections of the United States National Museum in Charge of the Smithsonian.* Smithsonian Contributions to Knowledge 22 (4).

Read, D. W. 1974. "Some Comments on Typologies in Archaeology and an Outline of a Methodology." *American Antiquity* 39: 216–242.

Rouse, I. B. 1939. *Prehistory in Haiti: A Study in Method.* Yale University Publications in Anthropology no. 21.

Sabloff, J. A., and G. R. Willey. 1980. *History of American Archaeology.* 2d ed. San Francisco: W. H. Freeman.

Sackett, J. 1985. "Style, Ethnicity, and Stone Tools." In *Status, Structure, and Stratification: Proceedings of the Sixteenth Annual Conference*, edited by M. Thompsen, M. T. Garcia, and F. J. Kinde, 277–282. Calgary: University of Calgary.

Spaulding, A. C. 1953. "Statistical Techniques for the Discovery of Artifact Types." *American Antiquity* 18: 305–313.

Spier, L. 1916. "New Data on the Trenton Argillite Culture." *American Anthropologist* 18: 181–189.

———. 1917. "An Outline for a Chronology of Zuñi Ruins." *American Museum of Natural History, Anthropological Papers* 18 (3).

———. 1918. "The Trenton Argillite Culture." *American Museum of Natural History, Anthropological Papers* 22 (4).

Squier, E. G., and E. H. Davis. 1848. *Ancient Monuments of the Mississippi Valley*. Smithsonian Contributions to Knowledge, No. 1.

Thomas, C. 1894. "Report of the Mound Explorations of the Bureau of Ethnology." *Twelfth Annual Report, Bureau of Ethnology, 1890–1891*, 1–742. Washington, D.C.: U.S. Government Printing Office.

Trigger, B. G. 1989. *A History of Archaeological Thought*. Cambridge: Cambridge University Press.

Uhle, F. M. 1907. "The Emeryville Shellmound." *University of California, Publications in American Archaeology and Ethnology* 7: 1–107.

Whallon, R. 1972. "A New Approach to Pottery Typology." *American Antiquity* 37: 13–33.

Wilson, T. 1889. "The Paleolithic Period in the District of Columbia." *American Anthropologist* 2: 235–240.

———. 1899. "Arrowheads, Spearheads, and Knives of Prehistoric Times." *Report of the United States National Museum for 1897*, pt. 1, 811–988.

Wissler, C. 1916. "The Application of Statistical Methods to the Data on the Trenton Argillite Culture." *American Anthropologist* 18: 190–197.

———. 1917. "The New Archaeology." *American Museum Journal* 17: 100–101.

Wyman, J. 1875. *Fresh-water Shell Mounds of the St. Johns River, Florida*. Peabody Academy of Science, Memoir 4. Salem, Mass.

3

Origins of Americanist Stratigraphic Excavation Methods

David L. Browman

One issue of continuing confusion in the study of the roots and development of Americanist archaeology is the question of the beginning of systemization of recovering of archaeological data through well-documented stratigraphic excavation techniques. I contest several claims that "everyone was doing it" or that such systemization was "widespread" by the last quarter of the nineteenth century. The confusion arises, I argue, from the disjunction between the use of post facto observations of stratigraphy in a completed excavation as a mechanism to assist in *interpreting* the artifacts salvaged, contrasted with a *contextual* approach that employs stratigraphic units a priori as the means of *recovering* artifacts in direct association or in context as part of a defined artificial or natural unit of stratigraphy.

The post facto interpretative approach was, in fact, widespread in the nineteenth century. Typically, it was achieved by the archaeologist going into the trench or other excavation unit at the end of the day, or at the end of the dig, trying to identify different stratigraphic levels in the remaining standing walls, assigning artifacts pulled out of the dig by the workmen to one or another level based on artifacts of that type or style seen in these walls, and employing this information in interpretation. Conscious or unconscious biases often influenced which stratum recovered artifacts were assigned to during analysis. Such post facto interpretation was practiced at least as early as the late seventeenth century (for example, by Olof Rudbeck in 1697).

In contrast, there was the method, first well developed by William Pengelly in the mid-nineteenth century, of explicitly recovering archaeological materials in context as part of the excavation procedure. This technique required materials to be rigorously recovered from, and kept with materials from, specific natural or artificial stratigraphical units defined during excavation, the kind of procedure that most students today assume when "stratigraphic excavation" is mentioned. This approach was implemented beginning in the late nineteenth century in America, and then only by a very few individuals; it did not become standard procedure until the first half of the twentieth century.

Americanist stratigraphic excavation developed from several intellectual links; early stratigraphic work in the Midwest and Northeast, for example, has a slightly different intellectual heritage than stratigraphic excavation procedures in the Southwest. Chains of evidence indicate that the ultimate roots of Americanist stratigraphic techniques can be traced back to William Pengelly, but that the technique entered the lexicon of Americanist archaeologists through different channels in the different regions of the United States.

European Roots

I believe that the development of more rigorous recovery techniques (for example, stratigraphic excavation) can be traced to the attempts by paleontologists, geologists, and archaeologists to settle the argument, in the nineteenth century, about whether humans were contemporary with extinct Pleistocene animals in Europe or whether humans only entered Europe after the last "Ice Age." I have seen in various recent sources at least a dozen claimants for individuals who had observed associations of extinct fauna with artifacts before 1858, and I am sure that there are many more than that. Two of the best known are Father John MacEnery in England and Jacques Boucher de Crèvecoeur de Perthes in France; in hindsight, we now accept their discoveries, but at the time, their recovery techniques were inadequate and open to question, so that skeptics dismissed their finds as unsubstantiated. In that sense, they had much the same problem that Jesse D. Figgins faced with the initial Folsom discovery; if you want to convince your colleagues that you have evidence to upset the conventional state of affairs, you need to have rigorously recovered and documented evidence, and you need to be able to demonstrate this to a cadre of skeptical experts.

William Pengelly worked in the same area of England as MacEnery; in fact, he later reexcavated Kent's Cavern. Pengelly believed he had found associations of extinct fauna with artifacts prior to the excavations he conducted at Brixham Cave in 1858 but was unable to convince his colleagues. Hence, when he was put in charge of Brixham Cave excavations—the first widely agreed-upon locus where human artifacts were found in association with extinct Pleistocene fauna—he supervised excavations employing a new technique. The testimony of all the associated scientists and observers (Browman 1997) makes it clear that it was Pengelly, and Pengelly alone, who suggested approaching the excavation with a new method. For the first time, a cave was *excavated* stratigraphically, with all materials from each stratum catalogued and kept together with all the other associated materials from that unit. Up until his project, the standard method of scientific excavation in caves had been to sink a vertical shaft through the deposits being studied to find the richest area of the cave, then to simply excavate all materials around that shaft as one composite recovery unit.

The initial report of clear association of human tools with extinct Pleistocene fauna at Brixham Cave were quickly verified as irrefutable, owing to Pengelly's stratigraphic recovery technique. British scientists realized that if the evidence of such associations was correct in Brixham, other previous reports might also be correct. Thus, within months of Pengelly's initial report, British scientists revisited Boucher de Perthes's sites in France and decided the associations of those materials were correct after all. They also visited and verified other previously disputed sites in Europe.

French paleontologist (later archaeologist) Albert Gaudry also visited Boucher de Perthes's sites with British scientists at that time. Stimulated by these events, he promptly conducted his own excavations in 1859 in this area, again verifying the associations (Browman 2002a: 199–200). Very soon thereafter, Gaudry and his student and later colleague, Pierre Marcellin Boule, began employing Pengelly's stratigraphic excavation technique in the caves they were excavating. It will be through the French adoption of Pengelly's cave excavation strategy, starting with Gaudry and Boule, that we can trace the most direct influence on techniques later employed in the United States.

Technology Transfer to the Americas

Pengelly fine-tuned his approach when he was put in charge of new excavations at Kent Cavern in the next decade. He was now laying out a grid system of 1-by-3-foot horizontal units, with vertical control maintained by a combination of natural strata and arbitrary 1-foot levels. He advocated continuing the excavations to at least 4 feet below the last artifact-bearing strata into presumed sterile units, to ensure that there were no more deeply buried units, and he gave each find a find number and recorded its three-dimensional position in his catalog.

American scientists interested in archaeology clearly were keeping abreast of the new trends in Europe. To help spread the information of new discoveries and techniques, the Smithsonian Institution published English translations of the works of Adolphe von Morlot (1861, 1863), who discussed the French version of Pengelly's stratigraphic excavation. In order to enhance the recovery of artifacts for their collections, the Smithsonian Institution also published instructions for potential donors on the best way to recover archaeological materials. Thus, George Gibbs (1862, [1863] 1867) incorporated Pengelly's method into his Smithsonian Institution instructions for proper cave excavations. For example, for caves he suggested that materials be excavated and recorded with "each layer being kept by itself," and that "every fragment of bone or other evidence of animal life should be preserved and marked with order of its succession in depth." For burial or shell-mound excavations, however, he still advocated the old post facto recovery method, only suggesting that in such excavations, notice should be made if there was any stratification visible in the side walls when work was completed, and if so, artifacts should be tied by depth to those levels (Browman 2002c: 244).

Thus it might seem that the technology transfer was made within a few years, from the first published reports in 1859 in Britain, to Gibbs's first new directives in 1862. But for the most part, American archaeologists either did not understand what was being suggested or found the old ways more expeditious, for Gibbs's suggestions were honored in the breach, rather than being followed. Even within the Smithsonian Institution, the method had not been clearly accepted, for in 1878, Joseph Henry (1878: 4) revised the instructions, advising readers that the proper way to excavate a site was "by sinking a shaft from the center of the apex, or by cutting a ditch on a level with the ground," essentially reverting to the pre-Pengelly methods. But within a few years, the next set of instructions issued by Charles Rau (1883: 481) returned to Pengelly's technique, suggesting that a cave deposit "should be entirely removed in sections, its stratification (if there is any) carefully noted, and the relative position of each discovered artifact noted." At least in theory, then, Smithsonian archaeologists were advocating the use of careful stratigraphic control in excavation of cave deposits by the third quarter of the nineteenth century, although they were less certain of the utility of this method for mound projects. In practice, however, this method was not actually employed by any Smithsonian archaeologists until the first quarter of the twentieth century.

The Peabody Museum Method and Chicago Method

The earliest sustained use of stratigraphic excavation as a recovery method was by the Peabody Museum of American Archaeology and Ethnology of Harvard University. Called by some of its adherents the *Peabody Museum method*, it was borrowed later by University of Chicago archaeologists and better known as the *Chicago method*.

The Peabody Museum method derives from the work of Frederic W. Putnam. Exactly how and when Putnam became an advocate of the method is still a matter of conjecture, as we have yet to locate a definitive statement from Putnam himself indicating how he happened upon the technique. One avenue that seems most likely is through his association with Jeffries Wyman, who was not only the first director of the Peabody Museum but also one of Putnam's three major instructors when he had trained at the Lawrence Scientific School at Harvard. The Lawrence Scientific School (1847–1906) was the only place at Harvard for advanced instruction in the sciences until 1871; Putnam entered in 1856 and continued his training there with Louis Agassiz, Asa Gray, and Jeffries Wyman until 1864 (Browman 2002b, 2002c).

From Putnam's own reports, we know that his first archaeological observations came in 1857, his second year as a student at Harvard, when he investigated the artifacts at a shell mound on the outskirts of Montreal while attending a meeting of the American Association for the Advancement of Sciences. The next explicit mention of archaeology comes from the period when Putnam was associated with the Essex Institute in Salem, Massachusetts. He was named first a curator, then director of the Essex Institute from 1864 to 1870, and when the Museum of the Peabody Academy of Sciences of Salem was formed out of a merger of the museums of the Essex Institute and the East India Marine Society, he became director of that museum from 1869 to 1873, in charge of archaeology among other duties. His first publication in archaeology was "On Indian Graves on Winter Island, Salem, 1865" in 1866, based on work carried out while at the Essex Institute. During the rest of his tenure there, he published 32 additional papers on various archaeological projects. Hence, before he was appointed to the Peabody Museum position, he had been involved in archaeological projects for at least a decade.

From publications of both Putnam and Wyman, we know that Putnam assisted Wyman in the excavation of various shell mounds near Eagle Hill, Ipswich, Massachusetts, in 1867 and so would have had the opportunity to learn at first hand in the field from Wyman. Wyman's interest in archaeology went back as early as 1846, when he began a correspondence with Ephraim Squier on mounds; the first published report of excavation work by Wyman is in 1852, and by the 1860s he was involved in multiple excavations in shell mounds in Maine, Massachusetts, and Florida. Wyman seems to have been very much influenced by the English translation of French methodology by Adolphe von Morlot, published in the 1861 Smithsonian Institution volume; he makes explicit reference to von Morlot's report in various papers published in 1867 and later. From secondary sources, and from Wyman's summaries, we know that he made careful notes on the strata and context from which artifacts derived, noting and recording changes in strata as they correlated with artifact category. To what extent he was employing the explicit stratigraphic excavation recovery techniques of Pengelly and the French is not yet clear.

As noted, Wyman would have had ample opportunity to pass on his ideas to Putnam. He had been one of Putnam's professors from 1856 to 1864, he was excavating shell mounds in Maine and Massachusetts by 1864 (Putnam 1875: 504), he and Putnam had excavated together in 1867, and Putnam and Wyman kept in active contact, by personal meetings and correspondence, until Wyman's death in 1874. Thus Wyman seems a reasonable, but as yet not definitively proven, vehicle for the introduction of Putnam to the ideas of stratigraphic recovery.

While Frederic Putnam directed students and researchers in American archaeology for nearly four decades, he was less than explicit in describing his method in his written reports, and we must in part use the statements of his students as proxies for what Putnam was doing and teaching. The investigation into the roots of Putnam's methodology is made more difficult because Putnam did not teach formal official courses in archaeology until 1890.

Between 1876 and 1890, Putnam employed two mechanisms for teaching or passing on his ideas on archaeological techniques: apprenticeship and Lyceum-type lectures. He had been trained in an informal, apprentice or mentor type of internship when he was a student at Harvard, which was still the typical method employed by his colleagues when he began at the Peabody Museum. One avenue of passing on his technique, therefore, was through what might be called his "first generation" of students, individuals who apprenticed themselves or became student assistants to Putnam, particularly in the 1880s. As discussed below, it is through one of these student apprentices, William Baker Nickerson, that Putnam's method was passed on to Chicago graduate students half a century later.

The other mechanism of the day was through a kind of Lyceum or Chautauqua public lecture. The first clues about Putnam's method are found in these public lectures, and in fact it is through a published summary of one of these lectures that we can actually demonstrate the specific technique Putnam utilized. For the first few years of Putnam's tenure as curator for the Peabody Museum, he seems to have focused upon the funding and construction of the first museum building. But by early 1880, he was able to shift from building concerns to education and methodology. In 1881, he reported giving lectures at several local institutions, as well as developing a course of lectures held in the Peabody Museum. Putnam (1882: 70–71) wrote, "The subjects to be discussed in this course are as follows: first the Mounds and their contents; second, the Pottery from the Mounds; third, Ancient and Modern Pueblos; fourth; Mexico and Central America; fifth; South America; sixth Ancient Peruvian Art." In addition, he reported (1882: 71), "I have also just concluded a free course of nine lectures before members of the classes for Private Collegiate Instruction for Women in Cambridge," introducing archaeology to the students of the school which later became Radcliffe.

The following year, Putnam (1883: 191) reported giving 25 lectures on archaeology. A short announcement in *Science* ("Proceedings" 1884) for 1883 noted that "Mr. F. W. Putnam, of the Peabody Museum, Cambridge, announces his readiness to give lectures on American archaeology, based upon the course delivered last year before the Lowell Institute." By 1885, Putnam was offering a series of 38 public lectures (Putnam 1886a), roughly divided into two coherent "courses," and a group of other stand-alone lectures. Of the 38 lectures, Putnam noted, "The first fifteen lectures are planned to give in a continuous course a review of the prehistoric peoples of America" (Browman 2000b: 218). Topics covered included lithics, pottery, metals, burial mounds, and other specific archaeological data types. The second course of 10 lectures approached the material from a different perspective, detailing the various periods of cultural evolution that Putnam saw in the Americas, from the first entry, through two phases of hunters and gatherers based on lithic types, to agricultural groups. The third group of 13 lectures included a range of topics, ranging from rock art to excavation methodology. Some of these lectures he worked up into small pamphlets that were put on sale at the museum (for example,

Remarks on Chipped Stone Implements, 1885, and *Conventionalism in Ancient American Art,* 1887).

Of specific importance for the argument in this chapter was lecture number 38, listed in a 1886 brochure as "The Proper Methods of Exploration," a lecture that appears to be the one described by an anonymous audience member at Johns Hopkins University on December 15, 1885, as being on the "methods of archaeological research in America." The anonymous correspondent reported:

> Trenching and slicing, he said, could be used to express in general terms the method followed in field work. For instance, in exploring a mound, a trench is first dug at the base of the mound. . . . The wall is the first section of the exploration, and its outlines should be drawn or photographed and its measurements noted. . . . After this first section is made, the work is carried on by slicing, or cutting down about a foot at a time, always keeping a vertical wall in front, the whole width of the mound. Each slice thus made is a section, and whenever the slightest change in the structure is noticed or any object found, that section should be drawn or photographed, and measured as at first, and the exact position noted of any object, ash bed, or change in the character of the structure of the mound (Putnam 1886b).

Putnam was employing this method in actual fieldwork at least by 1883, if not earlier. In report of his mound work for 1883, Putnam (1885: 6) noted, "What should be done before conclusions of importance can be drawn, is to make careful and thorough explorations of several of the group . . . by cutting trenches their whole length and width, and digging at least two feet below the surface on which the mound rests. . . . [They should be] systematically examined, by a series of trenches through each mound, and not simply by sinking a shaft in its centre." For his mound work in 1884, an anonymous correspondent for the annual meeting of the American Association for the Advancement of Sciences, reporting on the paper given by Putnam on his excavations at the Turner mound group in Ohio, noted ("Proceedings" 1884) that the "very careful manner in which the exploration had been carried out—the earth taken away and examined shovelful by shovelful—was shown, and the results of the work enumerated and illustrated by diagrams and photographs in great number." The report for the following year's meeting in 1885 noted ("Proceedings" 1885) that "Mr. F. W. Putnam gave some very practical and detailed directions as to the proper exploration of mounds, pleading earnestly for thorough work in all explorations, and illustrated its value by several examples from his own recent investigations." The 1887 report on his excavations at the Schmitz Mound in Ohio stated that "the work of exploration was begun by digging a straight trench down to the clay hard-pan across one edge of the mound and another on the opposite side. The mound was then cut down in slices, throwing the earth behind and always keeping a vertical wall in front."

Putnam proposed his first formal classes in methodology as part of the three-year graduate curriculum he submitted to the faculty of Arts and Sciences of the University at the meeting of October 8, 1890, which was approved December 9, 1890 (Putnam 1891: 98–99). Putnam's program required a good deal more rigor than other training programs of the period. Frederick Starr (1892: 291), writing about the developing field of anthropology in this country, quoted the following description of the initial graduate curriculum in anthropology from a Harvard brochure: "A course of special training in archaeology and technology, requiring three years for its completion, will be given by Professor Putnam. It will be carried on by work in the laboratory and museum, lectures, fieldwork, and exploration, and in the third year by some special research. The ability to use French and Spanish will be necessary. For this course a knowledge of elementary chemistry, geology, botany, zoology, drawing, and survey-ing is required, and courses in ancient history, ancient arts, and classical archaeology are recommended as useful." It was in this curriculum that Putnam then began formally teaching his field methodology, but as yet I have not found a specific syllabus or description of the precise field meth-odologies covered.

However, further information on Putnam's methods, both at mounds and in caves, can be gleaned from descriptions of his procedures by col-leagues and students, such as Otis Mason, Charles Peabody, Frank Russell, Charles Willoughby, and, particularly, William Baker Nickerson. It is from the 1885 report of Otis Mason, one of Putnam's colleagues, that we learn that in Putnam's procedure, "every ounce of earth [is] passed backward through a screen or sieve."

Charles C. Willoughby, a student trained by Putnam on his Ohio mound excavation projects, provides more information. When Wil-loughby undertook his own excavations of mounds in Maine in 1892, he reports that he employed the grid method advocated by Putnam, using a 10-foot grid at one site and a 12.5-foot grid at a second site. In his report of his 1894 season, Willoughby noted that "the ground to be explored

[was] taken off into sections ten feet square . . . [with] workmen throwing the earth behind them as they advanced, keeping a perpendicular wall of gravel in front," with all artifacts and features located in three-dimensional coordinates on the grid. While the verbal description in Willoughby's reports is somewhat scant, Putnam asked Willoughby to make a plaster model of his project to display at the 1893 World's Columbian Exposition in Chicago. Putnam (1898) observed that Willoughby's Maine excavations "work was so admirably carried out in accordance with the Museum methods, that it was decided to use the material from the Orland site to illustrate the 'Methods of Archaeological Research by the Peabody Museum,'" which was at the exposition. This model included scale stakes set on the 10-foot-square grid systems, details of the stratigraphic working faces, features, and the like (see Browman and Williams 2002, frontispiece). The 1893 exposition attendee would have found the exhibit referred to in the official catalog as the "Peabody Museum methods of exploration."

Charles Peabody was another student who was trained at Harvard by Putnam. In Peabody's report of his mound excavation work in Mississippi in 1901–1902, he recounted setting up a grid system dividing the mound into 5-foot squares. Within this grid system, the method was (Peabody 1904: 23) "that of making successive cuttings down to the level of the surrounding ground, and thus, by throwing the soil from each new cutting into that preceding, making possible a thorough examination of the distance excavated, yet leaving the ground more or less in its original condition. At each five feet, description of the wall of soil in front of the excavators were taken." Peabody further stated that "the system of excavation was that practiced by the Peabody Museum."

The above quotations clearly summarize Putnam's, or the Peabody Museum's, method for excavating mounds. Versions of the same technique also were employed in cave excavations. For example, Charles Peabody utilized a metric version of this grid system in his work in cave excavations in Missouri and North Carolina; in Missouri, he employed a 1-meter grid system, using letters and numbers on opposite right-angle axes, and excavated across the site in vertical sections, keeping running vertical profiles at each 1-meter grid line.

Frank Russell also received his archaeological training under Putnam and received a doctorate in 1898 at Harvard. Putnam then hired Russell to teach in the department. From a copy of the notes from an anonymous student, we know that on November 5, 1902, Russell told students in his introductory class in archaeology that the proper excavation procedure in caves required one to "divide the cave into blocks one foot deep and three foot square" (Browman 2002c: 250). Thus it appears that Putnam taught his students the Pengelly method, outlined earlier in this chapter, as the appropriate means to excavate cave deposits—a conclusion supported by both Charles Peabody's explicit reference to utilizing the Peabody Museum method in his cave excavation projects and Frank Russell's description of the method in lectures to his class.

It is to an earlier student, William Baker Nickerson (ca. 1860–1926), however, that many midwestern archaeologists must credit the origins of the excavation methodology known in more recent periods as the Chicago method. In the museum's annual report for 1885, Putnam wrote (1886: 494) that "for about a year Mr. W. B. Nickerson has been engaged as a volunteer assistant in field work for the Museum. In March 1885, he partly explored a group of burial mounds in the Fox River valley, near Elgin, Illinois. . . . Afterwards he was associated with the work in Ohio." Nickerson continued to work directly for Putnam in 1886, taking part in the excavations in Ohio under the direction of Metz and Putnam (Putnam 1888: 37), but during that year, he left his direct association with the Museum. Putnam (1887: 568) wrote:

Two of our former collaborators have been obliged for pecuniary causes to seek other fields of labor, and the loss of their assistance is one of the reasons that has led me to suggest the possibility of the foundation of a form of scholarships, by which means might be at hand for the support of deserving students or assistants. . . . The first called from us is Mr. Nickerson, a young man, who, during the time he was associated with us in our work of special explorations in the field, evinced an aptitude for archaeological research which I greatly regret could not have been further encouraged by providing a small salary for his support.

Nickerson spent the next decade at various jobs in Michigan and Illinois, but he wrote nearly every year to solicit financial support from Putnam to aid various excavation projects undertaken during his vacation times. Small amounts of funds were always given by Putnam, and the artifacts from these excavations thus were sent to the Peabody Museum.

Nickerson began a major excavation project in Jo Daviess County, Illinois, in 1895, and it is through his correspondence there that we again discover his debt to Putnam in terms of methodology. In a letter to Putnam on April 3, 1895, Nickerson detailed his preparations for excavation of mounds, double checking with Putnam to make sure that he understood the Peabody Museum procedures properly: "As I understand it, a mound should be taken down in the inverse of the order of its creation, when necessary, in order to understand the structure; trenching of course to find the strata and to obtain an occasional plan section. The Ohio experience gave me an insight into the use of the compass in locating and subsequent charting that is simply invaluable." He continued this review of what he understood to be proper excavation technique in his letter of October 29, 1895, in which he referred to the use of a grid system with right-angle axes, dividing the mound to be excavated into 5-foot sections, and subdividing each 5-foot section into four 15-by-15-inch blocks (Browman 2002c: 255–256).

Fay-Cooper Cole sent Paul S. Martin out as the graduate student director of the first University of Chicago archaeological excavations in Jo Daviess County in 1926. Cole himself had no previous training in archaeology, so he relied upon the training his students brought with them this first season. Martin had one season excavating a mound in Wisconsin using horse-drawn slips. It is clear from the field journal, that the first season's crew had little background and little experience; for example, during the first two weeks they wrote back to Dr. Cole several times, requesting basic Bureau of American Ethnology and Smithsonian Institution reports that covered the area—reports that the local townspeople knew about but the field crew did not know.

The townspeople repeatedly told them of the extensive work of William Nickerson, who had just died that spring, so that after a month, they decided to contact his widow. She turned over to Martin and Blackburn all of Nickerson's daily notes, sketches, maps, photos, plans, and unpublished reports, as well as a copy of a manuscript detailing Nickerson's work and excavation procedures in Jo Daviess County. Martin was electrified; he wrote, "A cursory examination of his notes, plans and final report were enough to convince us that he was a *most* careful worker— almost too careful—and very scientific. His method of digging mounds was modern as was all his work" (Martin and Blackburn 1926, field notes, Aug. 11, 1926).

Following the field survey of two months, an additional one month of excavation was planned in 1926. Martin (1927: 57–58) wrote:

In September all the students that were available were brought up to Galena and set to work to do actual excavating. Before work was started, however, there was held a general meeting to decide by what methods the mounds should be dug. Undercutting [the method

Martin had utilized in Wisconsin] was tried and found to be undesirable in that region where burials and artifacts may be situated at any
level. Trenching was also given a trial but used only when time began
to get short. The best method for the excavation of conical mounds
appeared to be the removal of dirt in horizontal and vertical
squares—staked out beforehand by means of a transit. A clean
"face" or wall from the floor upward was maintained as work pro-
gressed into the mound—so that the workers could see at any time
banding or stratification that might appear—or signs that assured
the finding of burials or artifacts.

This latter method was, of course, the Peabody Museum method, which
Martin had just learned about a few weeks earlier from Nickerson's materials (Browman 2002c: 258–262).

Nickerson's new methods, tested at the end of the first season in 1926,
were again employed during the second University of Chicago summer
field season. In a brief note on this second season, Cole (1929: 344) noted
that Chicago was now employing a new method in which ground plans
now "were made every five feet" so that all artifacts could be accurately
located. The next season the crew shifted from Nickerson's 15-inch units
to 6-inch units within the 5-foot grids—what was popularized in the
1930s as Cole's method or the Chicago method. Particularly because a
large number of the WPA projects of the 1930s were staffed by Cole's
students, and because his students, like Jimmy Griffin, went to places like
Michigan to teach, the Chicago version of the Peabody Museum method
was rapidly spread and became the standard midwestern methodology.

Committee on State Archaeological Surveys

Another overlooked vehicle for the dissemination of the Peabody Museum
method is the Committee on State Archaeological Surveys. The committee
noted in their brochure to all state societies and archaeologists that "one
of the best published statements of detailed procedure will be found in
Arthur C. Parker's 'An Erie Indian Village and burial site,'" and then went
on to detail the methodology described in his report (Wissler et al. 1923:
17). In addition, Parker was subsequently a keynote speaker at the 1929
Conference on Midwestern Archaeology, held in St. Louis, Missouri, once
again passing on his ideas to amateurs and professionals (Parker 1929).

What excavation methodology did Parker employ, and where did he
learn it? Parker had taken several special courses under Putnam between

1901 and 1903, and also trained in field excavations with another Putnam student, Mark Raymond Harrington, in 1903 and later (Parker 1910: 358; Ritchie 1977: 533). Thus it should come as no surprise that the excavation method he advocated (1907: 478–479), quoted in the 1923 report and passed on to his students such as William Ritchie, is Putnam's Peabody Museum method. While the Chicago method quickly acquired a name to distinguish it, Putnam was a self-effacing individual, and so his Peabody Museum method is rarely referred to by any specific designation and is thus easy to overlook.

Southwestern Stratigraphic Methods

Another thread of influence on excavation methodology, deriving from Pengelly via the French, seems to come into American archaeology from a slightly different direction than Putnam and the Peabody Museum. It derives from Albert Gaudry and Gabriel de Mortillet and individuals they trained, such as Pierre Marcellin Boule, Abbe Henri Breuil, and Hugo Obermaier. As noted, Gaudry picked up his ideas about stratigraphic excavation from his contact with British scientists who had worked with Pengelly, and the reports of Pengelly's excavations at Brixham and Kent Cavern, and seems to have integrated them into his own work fairly early on (Browman 2000a: 199–201). Gabriel de Mortillet is reported as actively teaching these methods as well in Paris to colleagues such as Boule and others as early 1880 to 1883 (Browman 1997).

In a roundabout way of getting at this thread of our story, let us first look at Henry Chapman Mercer. Mercer became very interested in searching for evidence of late Pleistocene human occupations in the Americas when he was working at the University Museum in Philadelphia from 1891 to 1897. He communicated extensively with Boule and Gaudry and spent six months in Europe visiting ongoing excavations and observing technique. When he returned and began cave explorations in the United States, he reported excavating the Port Kennedy site in Pennsylvania, 1894 to 1896, now with a new methodology, utilizing 1-foot horizontal levels, with each separate excavation unit being 3 feet square and 1 foot in depth (Browman 2000a: 193), precisely the method Pengelly first employed for caves.

The most explicit description of Mercer's methodology is contained in the report of his series of cave excavations in 1895 in the Yucatán of Mexico. In some of the caves he employed 6-inch artificial levels, in others, 1-foot levels. As well, he often clustered these artificial strata units into larger cultural strata units in his descriptions. He explicitly indicated that he removed the content of each horizontal layer before proceeding to the next and carefully recorded all cultural material in three-dimensional coordinates (Browman 2000a: 195).

Mercer had no students, so his adoption of European methods was not passed on directly to other Americanist archaeologists. So why discuss Mercer? Because I believe his training reflects the kind of training and exposure that Nels C. Nelson received in 1912 from the French-trained archaeologists Breuil and Obermaier, a pair of archaeologists who, like Mercer, received their instruction from Gaudry and Boule and their colleagues. It is, of course, Nelson and Alfred V. Kidder who are generally credited with beginning, and popularizing, stratigraphic excavating procedures in the American Southwest.

Nelson had not published or reported on any stratigraphic excavation methods during his earlier archaeological fieldwork in California. In his first season of work in the Galisteo Basin in New Mexico for the American Museum of Natural History 1912, he also failed to employ any explicit stratigraphic excavation techniques (Browman and Givens 1996: 83). However, at the end of the first season of work, the American Museum sent him to Spain to observe and excavate with Breuil and Obermaier, who were using the excavation techniques they had learned from Gaudry and de Mortillet, the same kind of procedures Mercer had learned from Gaudry and Boule two decades earlier. Immediately upon his return to the Southwest for his second field season, Nelson employed his first explicit stratigraphic excavation, utilizing artificial 1-foot levels in a test square (Nelson 1916: 165) and later expanding the method to his entire excavation, as well as other projects in Kentucky and Florida (Browman and Givens 1996: 84).

Kidder began employing a kind of natural stratigraphic unit, almost at the same time Nelson was experimenting with his artificial units. Because of one of the courses that Kidder listed as taking at Harvard was from George Reisner, Doug Givens and I (Browman and Givens 1996) have argued that Kidder likely derived his ideas of stratigraphy as practiced in Europe indirectly though Reisner's influence. Putnam was no longer actively teaching at Harvard by the time Kidder was a student, and it was not clear whether Kidder received any training in the Peabody Museum method from others of the faculty at Harvard. Thus in 1996, I felt that the most likely source of influence was via Reisner, as I was unaware of the often-unnamed method called here the Peabody Museum method that was being employed by the Peabody Museum staff, particularly Charles Peabody and Roland B. Dixon. Today I am more of a mind to suggest that

Kidder's use of stratigraphy derived from a combination of influences—Putnam's Peabody Museum methods being employed by the anthropology staff, in conjunction with, and as reinforced by, Kidder's class work on methods with Reisner.

For southwestern stratigraphic archaeology, then, the mechanisms of technology transfer comes from a clearly different intermediary in the case of Nelson, and a slightly different set of Harvard intermediaries in the case of Kidder, than we saw for the Midwest and Northeast. But the ultimate roots seem to be traceable back to Pengelly via other European intermediaries.

Final Remarks

While the development of stratigraphic excavation in the American Southwest has a seemingly different direct intellectual heritage than the application of the technique in the Northeast and Midwest, there are several commonalities. The earliest origins of the application of the stratigraphic recovery methods seem to derive ultimately from William Pengelly's pioneering work; the French seem to be very important intermediaries in popularizing the method; and there is a strong, and previously underappreciated, Peabody Museum component to the methods as practiced in the last decades of the nineteenth century and first decades of the twentieth century in the United States. It is clear that the decision to employ rigorously controlled and defined stratigraphic excavation units to *recover* archaeological materials was one that Americanist archaeologists began to implement only a substantial time after they began employing post facto stratigraphic observations to help *interpret* their finds.

References

Browman, D. L. 1997. "An Appreciation of Claude Warren and Susan Rose's 'William Pengelly's Techniques of Archaeological Excavation.'" *Bulletin for the History of Archaeology* 7 (2): 31–34.

———. 2002a. "Henry Chapman Mercer: Archaeologist and Cultural Historian." In *New Perspectives on the Origins of Americanist Archaeology*, edited by D. L. Browman and S. Williams, 185–208. Tuscaloosa: University of Alabama Press.

———. 2002b. "Frederic Ward Putnam: Contributions to the Development of Archaeological Institutions and Encouragement of Women Practitioners." In *New Perspectives on the Origins of Americanist Archaeology*, edited by D. L. Browman and S. Williams, 209–241. Tuscaloosa: University of Alabama Press.

———. 2002c. "Origins of Americanist Stratigraphic Excavation in North

America: The Peabody Museum Method and the Chicago Method." In *New Perspectives on the Origins of Americanist Archaeology*, edited by D. L. Browman and S. Williams, 242–264. Tuscaloosa: University of Alabama Press.

Browman, D. L., and D. Givens. 1996. "Stratigraphic Excavation: The First 'New Archaeology.'" *American Anthropologist* 98: 80–95.

Browman, D. L., and S. Williams, eds. 2002. *New Perspectives on the Origins of Americanist Archaeology*. Tuscaloosa: University of Alabama Press.

Cole, F. C. 1928. "The 1927 Season." *American Anthropologist* 30: 505–506.

———. 1929. "The 1928 Season." *American Anthropologist* 31: 344–345.

Gibbs, G. 1862. "Instructions for Archaeological Investigations in the United States." *Annual Report of the Smithsonian Institution for 1861*, 292–296. Washington, D.C.: Government Printing Office.

———. [1863] 1867. "Instruction for Research Relative to the Ethnology and Philology of America." *Smithsonian Miscellaneous Collections* 7 (11), no. 160. 60 pp. [Separately published in 1863; included in a volume published in 1867.]

Henry, J. 1878. "Circular in Reference to American Archaeology." *Smithsonian Miscellaneous Collections* 15 (9), no. 316. 15 pp.

Martin, P. S. 1927. "Archaeological Survey of Illinois." *Wisconsin Archaeologist* 6 (2): 56–58.

Martin, P. S., and J. F. Blackburn. 1926. "Illinois Archaeology." Unpublished University of Chicago Field Expedition notes, with cross-references for card index, maps, and photos. June 27, 1926 to August 28, 1926. Illinois State Museum Archives, Springfield.

Morlot, A. von, 1861. "General Views on Archaeology." *Annual Report of the Smithsonian Institution for 1860*, 284–343. Washington, D.C.: Government Printing Office.

———. 1863. "An Introductory Lecture to the Study of High Antiquity, Delivered at the Academy of Lausanne, Switzerland, on the 29th of November, 1860." *Annual Report of the Smithsonian Institution for 1862*, 303–317. Washington D.C.: Government Printing Office.

Nelson, N. C. 1916. "Chronology of the Tano Ruins, New Mexico." *American Anthropologist* 18: 159–180.

Parker, A. C. 1907. "Excavations in an Erie Indian Village and Burial Site at Ripley, Chautauqua Co., N.Y., Being the Record of the State Museum Archaeological Expedition of 1906." *New York State Museum Bulletin* 117: 459–554.

———. 1910. "Arthur Caswell Parker." In *American Men of Science*, 2d ed., edited by J. M. Cattell, 358. Lancaster: Science Press.

———. 1929. "The Value to the State of Archaeological Surveys." In *Report of the Conference on Midwestern Archaeology, Held in St. Louis, Missouri, May 18, 1929*, edited by F. C. Cole, 31–41. National Research Council Bulletin no. 74, Washington, D.C.

Peabody, Charles. 1904. "Explorations of Mounds, Coahoma County, Mississippi." *Papers of the Peabody Museum of American Archaeology and Ethnology* 3 (2): 21–64.

"Proceedings of the Section of Anthropology." 1884. *Science*, o.s., 5 (87): 342–346.

"Proceedings of the Section of Anthropology." 1885. *Science*, o.s., 6 (136): 230–234.

Putnam, F. W. 1866. "On the Indian Grave on Winter's Island, Salem, 1865." *Proceedings of the Boston Society of Natural History* 10: 246–247.

———. 1875. "Jeffries Wyman." *Proceedings of the American Academy of Arts and Sciences* 10: 496–505.

———. 1882. "Report of the Curator." *15th Annual Report of the Peabody Museum of American Anthropology and Ethnology*, 55–73.

———. 1883. "Report of the Curator." *16th Annual Report of the Peabody Museum of American Anthropology and Ethnology*, 159–192.

———. 1885. "Account of His Recent Excursions in Wisconsin and Ohio (1883)." *Proceedings of the American Antiquarian Society*, n.s., 3: 4–20.

———. 1886a. *Lectures on American Archaeology*. Cambridge: Peabody Museum of American Archaeology and Ethnology, Harvard University.

———. 1886b. "On Methods of Archaeological Research in America." *Johns Hopkins University Circulars* 5 (49): 89–92.

———. 1886c. "Report of the Curator." *19th Annual Report of the Peabody Museum of American Anthropology and Ethnology*, 477–501.

———. 1887. "Report of the Curator." *20th Annual Report of the Peabody Museum of American Anthropology and Ethnology*, 535–570.

———. 1888. "Report of the Curator." *21st Annual Report of the Peabody Museum of American Anthropology and Ethnology*, 11–16.

———. 1891. "Report of the Curator." *24th Annual Report of the Peabody Museum of American Anthropology and Ethnology*, 87–99.

———. 1898. "Editorial Note." In Prehistoric Burial Places in Maine, by C. C. Willoughby. *Archaeological and Ethnological Papers of the Peabody Museum* 1 (6): 387–388.

Rau, C. F. 1883. "Circular Relative to Contributions of Aboriginal Antiquities to the United States National Museum." *Proceedings of the United States National Museum* 6: 479–483. Washington, D.C.: Government Printing Office.

Ritchie, W. A. 1977. "Arthur Caswell Parker." *Dictionary of American Biography, Supplement 5*: 533–534. New York: Scribner.

Starr, F. 1892. "Anthropological Work in America." *Appleton's Popular Science Monthly* 41: 289–307.

Wissler, C., A. W. Butler, R. B. Dixon, F. W. Hodge, and B. Laufer. 1923. *State Archaeological Surveys: Suggestions in Method and Technique*. Washington, D.C.: Committee on State Archaeological Surveys, Division of Anthropology and Psychology, National Research Council.

4

Wissler's Gyroscope

Contexts for the Chronological Revolution

James E. Snead

The beginning of the second decade of this century was perceived by many in American archaeology as a time of crisis. One anthropologist, returning from a Washington meeting in 1912, reported that "Fewkes, Holmes, and others were lamenting the decline of archaeology in America in contrast to the very great advance in ethnology."[1] The achievements of the previous years, during which archaeology had increasingly become a part of the national scientific agenda, appeared to be aging along with the generation of scholars that had promoted it. In contrast, ethnology had been invigorated, in large part due to the efforts of Franz Boas and his students, and was expanding in influence. To those in the old power centers of archaeology in Washington, D.C., and New York, the waning of their influence in the face of the Boasian agenda was a troubling sign.

Only a decade later, however, archaeology was a thriving and reinvigorated discipline, owing primarily to the innovative archaeological work conducted in the American Southwest by a younger generation of anthropological archaeologists, in particular Nels Nelson, Alfred V. Kidder, Alfred L. Kroeber, and Leslie Spier. As participants in a multiyear program of southwestern research instituted by the American Museum of Natural History (AMNH), these scholars were at the forefront of a movement that emphasized the role of archaeology in documenting change over time. This effort transformed the orientation of archaeology in North America and became a central component of the culture history paradigm that was to dominate the discipline for 40 years.

In recent years, historians of archaeology have expressed considerable interest in the theoretical and methodological innovations of the 1910s, collectively referred to as the *chronological revolution*. In general, these historical studies have adopted one of two methods. The first emphasizes the history of archaeological approaches to chronology itself, particularly focusing on the origins of techniques of stratigraphic excavation.[2] The second strategy casts early chronological archaeology in largely theoretical terms, arguing that it was change in the perception of archaeological data, rather than necessarily the innovation of particular techniques, that was the critical contribution of Nelson, Kidder, and others.[3] In general, both approaches are based on the published works of the first generation of archaeologists interested in chronology and those of their mentors.

A third approach to the study of the chronological revolution is to establish its institutional context. As with other aspects of human society, the production of knowledge is the result of a range of factors, including class, ideology, education, politics, and economics, each of which constrains and molds opportunity for innovation. The institutional settings for research, the competition between scholars for funding and patronage, and the dynamic between professional and popularizing trends within disciplines are all key parameters in creating the context within which method and theory develop. In the absence of such a frame of reference, an understanding of paradigm shifts such as the chronological revolution necessarily remains limited.

The following discussion adopts such a contextual approach in the study of the origins and implementation of the Southwest archaeological work of the AMNH in the decade prior to World War I. Rather than published sources, principal reliance is placed on correspondence and memoranda produced by the participants in the project themselves, housed in archival collections at national and regional institutions. Of central concern are the actions and motivations of the two central figures in the chronological revolution at the AMNH, Clark Wissler and Nels Nelson. As anthropologists functioning within an evolving institutional context and subject to an array of social and intellectual influences, Wissler and Nelson made many of the decisions that produced the agenda for chronological archaeology. Exploration of that context, in turn, allows for a clearer picture of the forces that transformed American archaeology in the decade prior to World War I.

The Institutional Setting

The Department of Anthropology at the American Museum of Natural History was largely the creation of Frederic Ward Putnam, who in 1894 was recruited by the museum's president, Morris K. Jesup, to absent himself from his position at Harvard's Peabody Museum for one week a month to build a reputable anthropology program in New York. Over the next eight years the group of scholars assembled by Putnam and Franz Boas, who joined the department in late 1895, established the AMNH as a center of anthropological research on a par with the Bureau of American Ethnology (BAE) and the Peabody. Support from Jesup and an array of other prominent sponsors, such as Collis P. Huntington, Talbot Hyde, and the duc de Loubat, made possible a series of ethnographic and archaeological field expeditions within North America and further abroad.

This remarkable synthesis, however, began to come apart shortly after the turn of the century. Putnam and Boas had different visions of the future of American anthropology, and their deteriorating relationship was one reason for Putnam's departure from the AMNH in 1903.[4] Friction between Boas and members of the museum administration, particularly director Hermon Carey Bumpus, prevented him from taking full advantage of his new authority, and he felt compelled to leave the AMNH for Columbia in the summer of 1905.[5] In their wake, Putnam and Boas left a demoralized and divided department.

Boas was succeeded by Clark Wissler. Wissler, born in Indiana in 1870, had a background in pedagogy, coming to New York after several years teaching school in the Midwest.[6] He received a doctorate in psychology at Columbia in 1901 under James McKeen Cattell. In the process he also took courses with Boas and Livingston Farrand. In 1902, Boas, who described Wissler as a former student, recommended that the AMNH send him to conduct ethnographic fieldwork in the Dakotas.[7] When Boas resigned, it was Wissler who was given a temporary appointment to replace him. The position was made permanent shortly afterward, and Wissler maintained his affiliation with the AMNH until his death in 1947. The circumstances of his hiring appear to have permanently soured relations between Wissler and Boas, who preferred that a more senior scholar be assigned to the post he had vacated.[8]

In the beginning, Wissler's status was made precarious by poor health, lack of seniority, and complex institutional politics. At the request of President Jesup, effort was directed toward the museum's exhibition program rather than toward fieldwork.[9] Unlike his predecessors, Wissler built close relationships with members of the museum administration and soon could count on Hermon Bumpus as a close and vital ally. Jesup died in 1908; his successor, vertebrate paleontologist Henry Fairfield Osborn, shifted museum priorities away from anthropological expeditions.[10] Paradoxically, these adverse circumstances allowed Wissler to establish greater control over the Department of Anthropology, since the perceived indifference of an Osborn administration prompted most of the disaffected staff members to resign.[11] With only a small group of assistants remaining, Wissler was in a position to rebuild the department on his own terms.

In this regard his emphasis was quite different from that of his predecessors. Despite his own eclectic background, Wissler was committed to establishing anthropology at the AMNH as a professional, integrated discipline with ethnology at its center. The department's staff for the first decade of its existence had been composed largely of loosely affiliated scholar-entrepreneurs, such as Adolph Bandelier, or protégés of Putnam, most of whom were archaeologists with little advanced academic training. Fieldwork had been as much a matter of opportunity as of design. Patronage relationships had also intruded into the fabric of the department, blurring the line between institutional and personal loyalties. While Boas's advocacy of a more professional approach to anthropological research had resulted in some spectacular achievements, his inability to function within the institutional framework of the AMNH had hampered the effort. Wissler, whose political skills had been enhanced by years of low budgets and patient planning, was to have greater success. The program he began to establish in 1909 had four essential ingredients: increased levels of professionalism within the staff, clearer pathways of financial support for departmental projects, carefully nurtured institutional prerogatives, and an integrated approach to anthropological research that not only relied on each of the evolving subdisciplines but grounded them within the museum setting.

Each of these developments came to be reflected in the first major fieldwork effort to be promoted under the Osborn administration, what later came to be called the Huntington Southwest Survey. Although Wissler continued to conduct fieldwork on the High Plains, he seems to have been thoroughly aware of the anthropological possibilities of the southwestern United States. Southwestern research and the resultant collections had occupied a place of prestige within anthropology since at least the 1880s. Until 1909, however, activities of the AMNH in New Mexico and Arizona had been dominated by the personnel of the Hyde Exploring Expedition, which in the aftermath of their excavations at Chaco Canyon had conducted several less ambitious ventures elsewhere in the Southwest.[12] The activities of Talbot Hyde and George Pepper had initially fallen outside Wissler's jurisdiction, which seems to have prevented other museum efforts in the region. The departure of Pepper for the University of Pennsylvania in December 1908 removed this constraint, and Wissler acted quickly.

The Huntington Southwest Survey

In January 1909, while Pepper's resignation was still being processed, Wissler set about instituting a new program of research and hiring anthropologists to conduct it. He began with Herbert J. Spinden, a Harvard doctoral student who had recently conducted North American fieldwork for AMNH. "It would be his duty," wrote Wissler, "to work among the living tribes of the Southwest and to care for the archaeological collections from the same region."[13] This communication was followed on January 23 by a request to hire Pliny Earle Goddard, an established scholar at the University of California, as assistant curator.[14] Goddard specialized in the study of Athabaskan languages, and it was Wissler's intention to send him to conduct fieldwork among the Navajo and Apache. In filling these positions, Wissler demonstrated both his interests in professionalizing the department and in pursuing southwestern fieldwork.

Rather than emphasize detailed, long-term studies of particular culture groups as advocated by Boas, however, Wissler promoted cross-cultural research through the study of culture "traits."[15] Analysis of traits allowed for a focus on material objects, as Wissler wrote to director Bumpus: "We are giving our attention . . . chiefly to the material culture and the arts—partly because they have been neglected and partly because they are nearer the province of a museum."[16] Acquisition of collections was thus a high priority, and an aggressive exhibition program was also planned. Wissler demonstrated a grasp of the results-oriented viewpoint of the museum administration and possible patrons, his reports reflecting a concern with timely completion of field projects and the rapid public presentation of results. For the audience of professional anthropologists, Wissler's projects produced an extensive array of publications, in particular through the museum's Anthropological Papers series.[17] While the study of material culture was at the core of the research program, its success would promote research on related topics, such as Goddard's Athapaskan linguistics. In addition, Wissler, Goddard, and Spinden were all themselves academically trained anthropologists, linked by training or experience to the three teaching centers of Columbia, Harvard, and Berkeley. With this network the members of the museum's revived Southwest program were well positioned to make the planned program of research a success.

The timing of the proposed Southwest expedition also came at a fortu-

itous moment for the AMNH. In the wake of the Hyde Expedition's collapse, serious competition for the museum's preeminence in anthropology
in New York had begun to take shape through the ambitions of George G.
Heye. Heye had been building up a personal collection of Native American artifacts for several years and had coopted both George Pepper and
Marshall Saville, who had been the senior archaeologist at AMNH, into
his employ. The long process that was to lead to the establishment of the
Museum of the American Indian involved several rounds of negotiation
between Heye and the AMNH over the acquisition of Heye's collections.
These began in 1909 and had the avowed purpose of heading off the
creation of a rival institution.[18] Wissler's new project may have been perceived as a way to shore up the museum's local preeminence in anthropology in the face of competition. Funding, however, remained problematic,
particularly since the circumstances of Pepper's departure had effectively
cut off access to the network of funds that had supported Southwest work
in the past. With institutional support remaining limited, Wissler turned
to outside sources, ultimately attracting the patronage of one of the major
institutional donors of New York at the time, Archer Milton Huntington.

Huntington was the adopted son of the founder of the Central Pacific
Railroad, Collis P. Huntington.[19] He was born in 1870, and, while trained
to follow his father in business, ultimately devoted his life to other pur-
suits. By 1909, Huntington was a productive and active promoter of science and culture in New York City; he was also an ally of President
Osborn, who was attempting to make him a trustee of the museum. Despite his disinclination to favor anthropology, Osborn seems to have realized that cultural concerns were more important to Huntington than
strictly scientific matters, and he backed Wissler's efforts to gain Huntington's support for the new Southwest program. Huntington also became the point man in negotiations with George Heye.[20] His prestige
was thus firmly attached to the AMNH in general, and Wissler's new
research program in particular, in the face of rival interests. These events
seem to have been well under way at the time Spinden's hiring was
broached, and on June 6, 1909, with the receipt of a check in the amount
of $5,000 for the support of Southwest research, the new expedition came
into being.[21]

Huntington's contribution was administered by what was called the
Committee on the Primitive Peoples of the Southwest. With initially only
Huntington and fellow trustee James Douglas as members, the committee
served essentially as a conduit for the funding of Wissler's Southwest
projects. Reports that documented the progress of the research were peri-

odically issued. The first of these, in February 1910, tersely noted that "the collections received are most satisfactory demonstrations of the wisdom of this undertaking and assure the ultimate construction of an exhibition hall that will be architecturally attractive and of exceptional educational importance."[22] While the concerns of the trustees for the educational value of the work were thus addressed, the scientific work of the project proceeded. In Huntington, Wissler had a patron who, while steadfast in his financing, desired no direct role in its implementation.

In the meantime, Wissler continued to organize the project. Goddard had taken his position in the Department of Anthropology in early summer 1909 and began fieldwork among the Apache shortly thereafter. Spinden was in the field by early fall. In New Mexico he and Goddard were shortly joined by Wissler, who seems to have taken the opportunity for convalescence from an unspecified illness to make certain that the project was developing as he had planned.

For the rest of 1909 and the first half of 1910, Wissler was in the Southwest, traveling frequently and conducting ethnographic research of his own, while keeping an eye both on his two associates and on events back in New York. In his extensive correspondence with director Bumpus, Wissler described an environment new to him, in which the growth of Indian tourism and the activities of collectors created particular opportunities for a self-described "museum man." Detailed plans for the new Southwest exhibit were scribbled on note paper, with observations on the activities of rival field parties mounted by George Heye and by the Field Museum made from near at hand. During this period Wissler also turned his thoughts to conceptual issues, which were to be central to the activities of the Huntington Survey throughout its duration, in particular the study of chronology.

Wissler had an interest in archaeology, and had firm ideas about its role as an integral component of anthropological method. He expounded on this philosophy in a letter to Bumpus, which deserves to be quoted at length:

> Archaeology is not . . . a thing of itself; it is only a method of investigating cultures by the spade and the scoop. I am sorry to say that in America some, who ought to know better, think the whole thing is digging up pots and gloating over them (I admit that is not very much like anthropology). It is a method to be called in when you need it. . . . We need somewhere in America a long base line from the present to great antiquity by which to be guided, and to serve as a

gyroscope. How can we study cultures, without being able to trace one for an appreciable span?[23]

It was only through archaeology that the critical variable of time could be incorporated into ethnographic analysis, and the role of historic change was central to Wissler's ideas concerning culture areas. While this approach to the archaeological record could be broadly construed, Wissler's application was narrow: identifying changes in traits over time. Archaeology as anthropology was, simply, chronology. The fact that archaeology was not a part of the field plan for the first year is an indication that it was seen as playing a supportive, rather than central, role in Wissler's program. The integration of ethnographic and archaeological research that Wissler proposed also did not extend to his vision of the new Southwest exhibit hall at AMNH, which was to be devoted to living peoples.[24] Wissler's discussion of the potential for archaeological study, however, indicates that he had begun to plan for its future contribution.

Archaeological research in the Southwest was first proposed in the report submitted to the Committee on the Primitive Peoples of the Southwest at the end of 1910. By this time, both Spinden and Goddard had returned from their first field seasons, and the Southwest collections of the museum were rapidly expanding. The demands on existing staff, however, meant that no one with significant archaeological experience was available. Wissler was also placed at a disadvantage due to the resignation of Hermon Bumpus in the summer of 1910.[25] The loss was significant, for Bumpus had been both a supporter and a friend to Wissler. In his place, Osborn hired Frederick A. Lucas, who was a biologist sympathetic to Osborn's interests in evolutionary studies.[26] In order to make the case for hiring an archaeologist to Osborn and the new director, Wissler appears to have played on their professional proclivities.

Osborn's interests in archaeology, in keeping with his paleontological background, were largely restricted to the Old World Paleolithic. Both he and Lucas expressed concern that the Department of Anthropology had no exhibits on this topic or on physical anthropology, called *somatology* in the parlance of the day. Wissler seems to have suggested that the museum hire an archaeologist with expertise in this area, a person also expected to conduct fieldwork for the Southwest project. It is unclear whether Wissler was manipulating the ambitions of the administration to gain his own ends or whether he thought that the centrality of chronological issues to paleolithic studies would be appropriate training for the work he had in mind. The desired combination of skills, however, was to prove critical, both in the selection of a man for the position and for the course of his career. Wissler seems to have had no particular interest in Europe, but by committing himself to hiring someone who did, he was in effect giving Osborn a hand in directing the activities of the new hire. Between Wissler and Osborn, the new archaeologist would have two entrenched superiors whose expectations would be formidable.

Nels Nelson and the AMNH

The execution of the chronological program of the AMNH is most closely associated with Nels Nelson. Nelson's role in the methodological innovations of the Huntington Survey, however, is often misrepresented, a circumstance in part attributable to his limited publication record. Using Nelson's own correspondence, archived at the AMNH, a more nuanced version of his southwestern fieldwork and its legacy can be constructed.

Nels Christian Nelson was born on a farm near Fredericia, Denmark, and immigrated to the United States in 1892 to work on the farm of an aunt living in Minnesota.[27] There he learned English, attended school, and aspired to the ministry. Instead of attending a nearby college, however, Nelson traveled to California, where he worked various jobs until gaining admission to Stanford. He switched to the University of California shortly afterward. There he gradually turned from the study of philosophy toward anthropology, which he described as having a scope "as wide as human nature itself. . . . It calls into play, as no other field, every faculty of the mind."[28]

It is often presumed that Nelson's principal mentor at the University of California was Alfred Kroeber. Kroeber had been on the faculty of the Department of Anthropology at Berkeley since its inception in 1901, working under the absentee directorship of Frederic Putnam until Putnam's retirement in 1909.[29] He was the central figure in the department for decades thereafter. In this early period, however, his role in the promotion of California archaeology, and the careers of such developing archaeologists as Nels Nelson, seems to have been secondary to those of others in the university, in particular geologist John Campbell Merriam. Merriam, a vertebrate paleontologist by training, had by the first decade of the century established himself as a national authority in his field.[30] His interests, however, encompassed archaeology, and he seems to have been the principal promoter of research on the shell mounds of San Francisco Bay, begun at a time when Kroeber was only beginning to establish himself in the area. Merriam was the motivating force behind Max Uhle's excavations of the Emeryville Shell Mound and sponsored work on the West Berkeley Shell Mound in the same year.[31] Given his particular background and interest in stratigraphic relationships, it is not unlikely that Merriam conveyed some regard for these issues to his colleagues and students.[32] The role of Merriam in the stimulation of stratigraphic "thinking" in American archaeology has yet to be seriously examined, but it is clear that his organizational role in the promotion of Uhle's, and later Nelson's, field-work was quite important.

Nelson, in fact, appears to have served as Merriam's major "field man" on shell-mound projects almost from the point of his arrival at the University of California. Correspondence from January 1906 describes archaeological reconnaissance in northern California conducted by Nelson on Merriam's behalf, what appears to have been the first of many such efforts conducted over the next several years.[33] Nelson's letters to Merriam indicate, among other things, recognition of and interest in archaeological stratigraphy, a concern that is evident in his published work on the subject as well.[34] While Nelson was also in regular contact with Kroeber, Merriam seems to have had the preeminent role in the shell-mound work. "I have asked Dr. K. to arm me with a brief 'to whom it may concern' letter," wrote Nelson, "which perhaps you ought to sign—especially if you are better known hereabouts than Dr. Kroeber."[35] Kroeber, however, seems to have gradually taken on a greater role both in the shell-mound work and in promoting Nelson's career. In 1910, Nelson and T. T. Waterman were hired as instructors and assistant curators at the University of California. The two men were to be rotated between the department at Berkeley and the museum, which at that time was housed in San Francisco.[36]

It was about this time that Nelson came to the attention of Clark Wissler. A dense network of professional ties linked the Department of Anthropology at the University of California with the AMNH. Both Boas and Putnam, Kroeber's former teacher and supervisor, respectively, maintained their interests in the AMNH despite having each departed the institution. Kroeber inherited this interest and worked in association with the AMNH several times during the course of his career. Merriam appears to have been a colleague of President Osborn's and spent the summer at the AMNH in 1907.[37] Pliny Goddard had worked in association with Nelson while at Berkeley, and he continued to correspond with him after his departure for New York.[38] When Wissler began his search for an archaeologist that could juggle the complex requirements mandated by the expanding programs of the AMNH, students of Merriam and Kroeber had high visibility.

The resignation of the sole remaining archaeologist at the AMNH, Harlan Smith, in September 1911 allowed Wissler to proceed in his efforts to hire new staff. In keeping with efforts to bring someone with expertise in the European Paleolithic, some interest was expressed in hiring the more established scholar George Grant MacCurdy for the post.[39] Goddard, however, vigorously promoted Nelson, whom he described as having interests "directed particularly toward the antiquity of man in Europe and man's relation to the lower animals. . . . He seems to me the most available man considering all the requirements involved to fill our long needed want of a man to bridge over the gap between the biological and anthropological exhibits and activities in the Museum."[40]

Osborn received a favorable report on Nelson from Merriam in June 1911. Nelson spent the same summer visiting museum collections in Europe, apparently to shore up his credentials in this area.[41] In contrast, it appears that little concern was expressed for Nelson's lack of familiarity with the American Southwest, a region he had visited only once, while on a lecture tour for the Archaeological Institute of America.[42] His general skills and museum experience, however, combined with what Goddard called Nelson's "high ideals and great perseverance"[43] were the necessary qualifications. It is also probable that the shell-mound excavations were perceived as ideal training for the chronological work that Wissler intended Nelson to pursue. Kroeber's initial response to the idea was negative, but arrangements were eventually completed for Nelson to take to the field in New Mexico on behalf of the AMNH by June 1, 1912.[44] Nearly three years after mentioning the subject to Hermon Bumpus, Wissler was to finally get archaeology formally incorporated into the agenda of the Huntington Southwest Survey, and he began the effort of establishing the chronological "baseline" upon which the comparative, ethnographic studies already under way were to be grounded.

San Cristóbal and Castillo Cave

Nelson's experiences in the years between 1912 and 1914 established the pattern of fieldwork that characterized the most productive years of his career. In keeping with the approach he had adopted in California, he began his southwestern work by conducting a regional survey, visiting sites and talking to local people along Rio Grande between El Paso and Santa Fe. In this he was accompanied by his wife, Ethelyn Nelson.[45] The Nelsons arrived in Santa Fe in early July, where they were joined by Clark Wissler. In his efforts to identify an appropriate site for the Huntington

Survey's excavations, Wissler had consulted with a variety of scholars, including Spinden and the young Alfred V. Kidder, but apparently wanted to go over the ground himself.[46] He may also have toured sites in the vicinity on his previous visit to the area in 1909.[47] In addition, Santa Fe was the location of the School of American Archaeology, which, under its director Edgar Lee Hewett, was the center for most locally based archaeology in the region. In his negotiations with Hewett and his oversight of Nelson, Wissler was exerting his authority as director of the expedition. Nelson does not seem thereafter to have dealt with Hewett directly himself, although Sylvanus Morley, on the staff of the school, visited the excavations along with Kidder late in the season.[48]

Upon his departure, Wissler left Nelson with a set of detailed instructions, requesting him to "excavate and investigate the site known as San Cristobal," located in the Galisteo Basin immediately south of Santa Fe.[49] The described purpose of the project had little direct relevance to chronological questions and was oriented toward assembling information on cultural traits in the vicinity. Nelson, with no evident background in excavating architectural sites, was dismayed by the size and complexity of San Cristóbal.[50] Surface indications proved no clear guide to the arrangement of buried walls, requiring care that the untrained workmen were not accustomed to. Despite this, work proceeded at great speed, with 262 rooms excavated between July 29 and September 8. In spite of his instructions, Nelson's reports on San Cristóbal were largely restricted to chronological interpretation based on the superposition of features, and even while he had yet to develop enough knowledge about the local ceramic types to discuss other sources of chronological data, it was the history of the site to which he directed his attention. The actual methods adopted by Nelson during his first season varied only moderately from those of contemporaries working elsewhere in the Southwest, the difference resting largely in its application rather than its conduct. Nelson arrived in New York in December 1912 to formally take up his post at the AMNH and to evaluate the fruit of a productive field season.

While Nelson had been grappling with the complexities of San Cristóbal, AMNH president Osborn had been making a tour of southern Europe in the company of George Grant MacCurdy. Osborn and Mac-Curdy visited many of the primary cave sites in France and Spain, including Tuc d'Audoubert, which had been discovered only days earlier. Their guides at these locations were some of Europe's premier archaeologists, such as the Abbé Breuil. In Spain they were particularly impressed with Castillo Cave, being excavated by Breuil and Hugo Obermaier.

Osborn had long been developing plans for the expansion of the museum's exhibits on human evolution, and his interest in Castillo Cave was directly related to the creation of displays that would portray human evolution in the museum's halls in the fashion that were already in place for other elements of the animal kingdom. Osborn's three-week foray into the European Paleolithic, which was to provide the subject of the 1914 Hitchcock Lectures at the University of California and in 1915 his *Men of the Old Stone Age,* would have a significant impact on Nelson's career, and, indirectly, on chronological archaeology.[51] Nelson, who was delegated to the project shortly after his return from the Southwest, seems to have approached it with little enthusiasm:

> The original plan as to remove a column of the material [from Castillo Cave] for Museum exhibition, but I believe Obermaier would not even allow that, as the column might conceivably contain valuable specimens. Personally I was unable to see anything of great value in such an unwieldy column, and furthermore I felt that Osborn's enthusiasm would probably subside in time and therefore I was not particularly anxious to go on a mission which seemed bound to be more or less of a failure. The plan now proposed is to watch Obermaier's operations for awhile and to get the necessary measurements, etc. for reproduction of his cave, as well as some type specimens, and then to make a round of some of the more important stations to get some first hand information on the whole palaeolithic problem and the manner in which it is being handled by the men on the spot.[52]

At no time does Osborn appear to have contemplated involving the museum in original field research in the European Paleolithic, and it is clear that Nelson was sent to Europe in 1913 purely to bolster the educational programs of the AMNH. He reached Puente Viesgo, a town in the Spanish province of Santander nearest Castillo Cave, prior to the nineteenth of May, remaining there until the middle of July.[53] Thereafter Nelson traveled through western Europe visiting sites and museums, returning to New York in late September.

The excavations at Castillo Cave have been perceived by scholars as a critical juncture between European and American archaeologies. While such a synthesis may have taken place, Nelson's actual reports from the summer of 1913 depict conditions that were less than ideal. "In fact," he wrote Wissler, "the whole thing looks more like a rock quarry than anything else. Blasting is continually necessary." In a later note, Nelson observed that collecting data for Osborn's model was difficult, due to "the fact that the different strata are not well enough differentiated, as to color and composition. In general the culture strata are black or dark in color owing to carbonized remains; but they are not invariably black, being sometimes not distinguishable from the sterile layers of debris composed of yellow clay and angular rocks. When the material [has] dried out the appearance of a model section will be even more dull & monotonous and uninteresting."[54]

Nelson, in later life, did consider his work with Obermaier as formative in his perception of stratigraphy, but it is difficult to detect this influence in his writings at the time.[55] Interestingly, modern researchers accord Nelson an important role in preparing the drawings of the stratigraphic sections at Castillo Cave in 1913, which suggests a more active role in the project than often credited.[56] His observation that there was little visual distinction in the Castillo Cave strata despite obvious changes in artifact style may have provided the stimulus for the innovation of artificial "levels" with which he is famously associated.

Nelson was able to spend the fall of 1913 in New Mexico, pressing westward almost immediately following his return to New York. The pattern of research in the 1913 season showed no signs of any new "influence," following instead the model of reconnaissance, architectural excavation, and mapping adopted in 1912. At this stage Nelson was already feeling the strain of meeting the expectations of both Wissler and Osborn, whose different agendas were making it difficult for him to carry out cohesive research.[57]

It was not, in fact, until the end of 1914, following a third Southwest field season, that Nelson conducted the single excavation for which he is most famous. Even this seems to have been almost an afterthought, coming after the publication of his major report on the Galisteo Basin pueblos and the excavation of hundreds of rooms at other sites in the region.[58] At some point between November 12 and 26, Nelson returned to San Cristóbal for one more week of excavation. The circumstances are obscure, since by that point he had ceased writing regularly in his field journal. Nelson had revisited the site more than once that summer and may have been searching for the proper location in which to attempt a stratigraphic experiment. Several cuts had been made in the San Cristóbal refuse heaps in 1912, and it was to these deposits that Nelson returned at the end of 1914: "Nearly all of last week was spent on the Pankey ranch, where with my own hands, I tried out a 3 ½ x 6 ½ ft. section to 10 ft. deep—of the largest refuse heap. The results are data (of a nature suitable for graphic illustration) showing three successive stages of pottery making."[59]

The significance of this find was that the ordering of the different pottery types meant that their relative ages could be established, setting up a chronology that could be applied to other sites in the region. San Cristóbal thus provided the "gyroscope" that Wissler had described five years earlier. Nelson was aware of the significance of this discovery from the outset. His emphasis on its suitability for "graphic illustration" suggests that the excavation in the San Cristóbal refuse dump was essentially the final piece of a carefully assembled argument, one that would make the case to a broader audience. In fact, his published article on the subject indicates that the chronological relationships established at San Cristóbal had been hinted at by discoveries earlier in 1914 at San Pedro Viejo, where historic and prehistoric segments of the site had been distinguished from each other.[60]

Nelson's subsequent article on Tano chronology, in fact, is more about ceramics than stratigraphy.[61] Through the patient, methodical reconnaissance that Nelson had made throughout the Rio Grande country, it seems to have been his observance of potsherds on the surface, and his awareness of variation in them, that led to the search for some place where stratigraphic control could be established. Nelson was interested in putting that most common form of archaeological data to use, a quest that was hampered by the scarcity of deep deposits in the Rio Grande pueblo ruins and Nelson's own belief that refuse deposits would be places "where grave diggers in overturning the debris again and again had surely destroyed the planes of stratification."[62] Upon finding a deposit that was deep and apparently undisturbed, Nelson organized stratigraphic units where none were apparent by excavating in 1-foot "spits," within which the frequency of different types of ceramics could be tabulated and compared to those of layers higher and lower. The waxing and waning of styles over time was thus evident, indicating a general chronological sequence of ceramics, which Nelson immediately used to assign relative dates to all of the sites he had visited.[63] Ultimately, the chronological innovations in the Southwest hinged on a sound grasp of regional archaeology, awareness of variation in ceramic style, and a realization that change could be manifest even in the absence of visually stratified deposits.

Conclusion: Consolidation and Advance

In addition to their strictly methodological impact, Nelson's San Cristóbal excavations provided impetus for the expansion of the entire southwestern chronological program. Recognition of the value of Nelson's innovation was rapid and widespread among the scientific community, enhancing the prestige of the anthropology programs of the AMNH.[64] This process was carefully orchestrated by Wissler. In January 1915, he wrote to Huntington, describing the development as providing the key to the understanding of Southwest prehistory, at the same time using it to implicitly underline the need for further funding.[65] Wissler was at the time embroiled in a dispute over disposition of a bequest left the museum by Morris K. Jesup's widow, which Wissler had anticipated would be in part devoted to the support of the anthropological projects that Jesup had favored. Osborn, however, had his own ideas as to how the money would be spent, and the experience seems to have left Wissler even more determined to build his own base of fiscal support.[66]

The project began to expand almost immediately. In March 1915, Wissler entered into an agreement with Livingston Farrand, who had departed Columbia and was serving as president of the University of Colorado, to conduct joint archaeological work in the La Plata district of southwestern Colorado.[67] Earl Morris was to be the "field man" for this effort. It was also during this period that Wissler began corresponding with A. E. Douglass, of the University of Arizona, concerning the possible archaeological applications of dendrochronology.[68] The ethnographic side of the Huntington Survey continued with the dispatch of Robert Lowie to the Hopi mesas in the summer of 1915 to collect data on kinship. Wissler wanted similar information from the pueblo of Zuñi; the assignment went to A. L. Kroeber, who had written the AMNH offering to conduct fieldwork during an upcoming leave of absence.[69]

These varied obligations placed Nelson in a "middle management" position. Wissler maintained direct authority over the various aspects of the Huntington Survey but relied on Nelson to keep tabs on the burgeoning archaeological activities as well as conduct his own fieldwork, which continued in 1915 and was extended to include a new effort at Chaco Canyon. Nelson was also by this time the only archaeologist at the AMNH, with responsibility to maintain all associated collections and exhibits.

The situation was further complicated by Kroeber's unanticipated entry into the field of archaeological chronology. Nelson had spent a month in Berkeley in the spring of 1915 writing up some of his old shell-mound reports and apparently had brought Kroeber up to date on the progress that was being made in assigning relative dates to southwestern sites. At the completion of his Zuñi season three months later, Kroeber announced that he had completed a chronological project of his own, based on the study of potsherds on sites in the Zuñi area. "I believe you will think I have built high on a narrow foundation," he wrote Wissler. "I have. But outside of Nelson no one has yet really tackled the archaeological problem of the Southwest . . . and I want at least to crack the ice."[70] Wissler's response to this development was cautious, in part due to the fact that Kroeber's primary loyalties were perceived to be to the University of California. "He has gone into the subject a little deeper than I anticipated," Wissler wrote Nelson, "and perhaps has skinned most of the cream off of this milk."[71] Kroeber's work was evaluated as "preliminary," with Wissler suggesting that the AMNH would investigate further the following year by inaugurating an excavation project at Zuñi.[72] However begrudgingly, the scientific importance of the Zuñi study was recognized and rapidly published.[73]

The year 1915 was a critical turning point for the Huntington Survey. The chronological insights that had been provided by Nelson's San Cristóbal excavations created an opportunity to focus on the broader range of chronological problems and the relationships of sites. Institutionally, however, what had been a focused, manageable project had become much more complex, with the Kroeber-inspired Zuñi work, Morris's La Plata project, and the evolving plans for Chaco Canyon all competing for attention. Even while Kroeber and Lowie provided new ethnographic data, Wissler continued to shift the emphasis of the Huntington Survey toward archaeology. Now that the chronological project was bearing fruit, he was intent on using it to enhance the prestige of his department and institution. The subsequent accomplishments of Leslie Spier in the Zuñi, Ramah, and Little Colorado Districts and of Earl Morris at Aztec Ruin were products of this drive to consolidate the role of the AMNH in shaping an agenda for American archaeology. In this regard, the museum found itself in direct competition with other archaeological interests that were attracted to the Southwest field, such as the Heye Foundation's work at Hawikuh and the developing interest of the BAE at Chaco Canyon.

This shift in emphasis toward archaeology, ironically, had a negative impact on Nels Nelson's own work. Increasingly required to spend his time in the Southwest monitoring the museum's other efforts rather than working on his own projects, his professional output shrank rapidly. The kind of problem-based, long-term research that had been so successful in the Galisteo Basin was not encouraged under the increasingly results-oriented and more competitive research environment four years later. Wissler's continued oversight from New York also limited Nelson's authority in the field. Spier seems to have sensed this jumbled chain of command and as a result acted largely out of his own initiative. Morris followed suit at Aztec, a project that Nelson took a dim view of from the start. Funding became increasingly contentious. Wissler's failure to attract the support of J. P. Morgan for the Aztec work beyond the first season meant that an increasing percentage of Huntington's annual appropriation was devoted to supporting Morris. "I should never have consented to letting the venture be started could I have foreseen several of the things that have happened," Nelson wrote Morris some years later.[74] Buried in routine work at the museum, and with minimal access to research opportunities, he grew increasingly bitter, an emotion expressed mainly through letters to colleagues at other institutions. By the time the entry of the United States into World War I terminated all of the Huntington Survey's work except for the Aztec project, Nelson's active participation in Southwest archaeology had come to an end.

By the early 1920s, however, the influence of the chronological studies initiated by Wissler and Nelson were already widely influential in Southwest archaeology. Both men were invited to attend the symposium assembled by BAE archaeologist Neil Judd at Chaco Canyon in 1921, at which chronology was a major topic of conversation. Neither attended, but both sent written statements that are good indicators of their personal attitudes and contributions toward the chronological revolution they had begun. Nelson confined his remarks to the issues at hand, summarizing the results of his regional reconnaissance, his disappointment at failing to obtain chronological data during his own work at Pueblo Bonito, and his hopes that Judd's work would provide solutions to these and related problems.[75]

Wissler, in contrast, took the higher ground, tracing the interest in chronology back to Putnam and emphasizing the centrality of the subject to American archaeology: "Without a true time perspective the data of our subject will be a chaos of facts from which the genuine reader and even the student will flee as from a pestilence."[76] Collectively, the statements of the two men, ostensibly read aloud at Judd's campfire in 1921, reflect the contrasting emphases of theoretical orientation and focused fieldwork that were the hallmarks of chronological archaeology in its initial stages.

The fact that neither Wissler or Nelson were there to deliver them in person was symbolic of the end of the active role of the AMNH in the chronological work it had begun.

The context within which the chronological revolution developed was thus far more complex than the published records of any of those involved indicate. Wissler's drive to professionalize the department and to conduct integrated anthropological research took shape in an environment of competition within and between institutions for funding and prestige. An awareness of the potential contribution of archaeology in providing a chronological framework for studies of culture traits preceded by some time its successful implementation. The method itself was more the outcome of Nelson's patient fieldwork than a bold methodological stroke, but its significance was immediately recognized and touted as a triumph for the institution. Wissler's active promotion, in fact, may have been the factor distinguishing the Southwest work of the AMNH from other contemporary and preceding projects that recognized chronological aspects of archaeological data. While a grasp of the concept of stratigraphy and a concern for the nature of change in archaeological data clearly informed Nelson's innovations, it was the context within which the project developed and was promoted, by Wissler's subtle hand, that provided the framework within which they were applied.

Author's Note

Much of the material in this paper is presented at greater length in Snead (2001). Since the data referred to in this chapter consist principally of correspondence and similar primary source material, notes are used instead of in-text citations.

Notes

1. Clark Wissler to Nels Nelson, January 8, 1912, Correspondence files, Anthropology Archives, Department of Anthropology, American Museum of Natural History (hereafter cited as Correspondence files, Anthropology Archives, AMNH).

2. Praetzellis 1993; Browman and Givens 1996; Willey and Sabloff 1993.

3. Lyman et al. 1997: 44.

4. Frederic W. Putnam to Morris K. Jesup, December 10, 1903, Frederic W. Putnam Papers, Harvard University Archives (hereafter cited as Putnam Papers).

5. Franz Boas to Morris K. Jesup, May 23, 1905, Correspondence files, Anthropology Archives, AMNH.

6. This discussion of Wissler's background is derived from Freed and Freed (1992).

7. Franz Boas to Hermon C. Bumpus, May 16, 1902, Correspondence files, Anthropology Archives, AMNH.

8. At various times in 1905 Boas had suggested bringing in either A. L. Kroeber or A. M. Tozzer as curator. Franz Boas to Morris K. Jesup, February 3, 1905, and Franz Boas to Hermon C. Bumpus, February 21, 1905, both ibid.

9. Clark Wissler to Henry F. Osborn, report (ca. 1915), Central Archives, American Museum of Natural History (hereafter cited as Central Archives, AMNH).

10. Kennedy 1968: 163; Rainger 1991.

11. George Pepper, who was in charge of the collections excavated at Pueblo Bonito by the Hyde Exploring Expedition, left for the University of Pennsylvania in late 1908; Marshall Saville, who had resigned in 1907 but remained as honorary curator, left permanently in January 1910. Snead 1997; Marshall Saville to Henry F. Osborn, January 19, 1910, Central Archives, AMNH.

12. Snead 1999.

13. Clark Wissler to Hermon C. Bumpus, January 2, 1909, Central Archives, AMNH. Spinden himself was kept in the dark about the project to which he would be assigned. Throughout the spring of 1909, he seems to have had the impression he was being hired to conduct ethnographic research among the Nez Perce, completing a project he had begun for the museum the previous summer.

14. Clark Wissler to Hermon C. Bumpus, January 23, 1909, ibid.

15. Freed and Freed 1983: 812.

16. Clark Wissler to Hermon C. Bumpus, December 23, 1909, Central Archives, AMNH.

17. Freed and Freed 1983: 810.

18. Awareness of the threat implied by Heye's activities is evident in a letter from Osborn to Archer Huntington, dated November 10, 1909 (Central Archives, AMNH), in which Osborn expresses his intent to support the Department of Anthropology.

19. Proske 1963.

20. Henry F. Osborn to Archer M. Huntington, March 2, May 1, 1909, Central Archives, AMNH.

21. Archer M. Huntington, subscriptions, ibid.

22. Report of Committees on Primitive Peoples of the Southwest, Annual Meeting of Board of Trustees, February 14, 1910, ibid.

23. Clark Wissler to Hermon C. Bumpus, December 24, 1909, ibid. Note that this comment precedes by several years the oft-cited remarks of Berthold Laufer (1913) on the need for archaeology to embrace the subject of chronology.

24. Clark Wissler to Hermon C. Bumpus, November 20, 1909, Central Archives, AMNH.

25. Newspaper accounts of the episode suggest that Bumpus's efforts to popu-

larize the museum had led to his downfall, but internal sources indicate that he had accused President Osborn of financial impropriety and was repudiated by the board of trustees. Undated newspaper clipping, Bumpus biographical file, ibid.; Kennedy 1968: 171.

26. Kennedy 1968: 172.

27. Data on Nelson's early life derived from Barton 1941. While Nelson's own personal files are archived at the AMNH, he edited them severely in the 1940s, apparently discarding all but a selection of the material bearing on his career prior to his involvement with the museum.

28. Nels C. Nelson to Earl M. Wilbur, July 4, 1907, Nels Nelson Papers, Archives, Department of Anthropology, American Museum of Natural History (hereafter cited as Nels Nelson Papers).

29. Frederic W. Putnam to Benjamin Ide Wheeler, May 8, 1909, Putnam Papers.

30. Stock 1938.

31. Rowe 1954: 8; Wallace and Lathrap 1975: 3. While it has been suggested that Nelson worked with Uhle (Praetzellis 1993: 73), Uhle had departed Berkeley for Peru in 1903, years before Nelson's arrival at the university.

32. Stock 1938: 769.

33. Nels Nelson to J. C. Merriam, January 4, 1906, J. C. Merriam Papers, Bancroft Library, University of California, Berkeley (hereafter cited as Merriam Papers).

34. Nelson remarks, for instance, that in the Ellis Landing Shell Mound, "no stratification occurs beyond what the overabundance of the different species of shell produce." Nels Nelson to J. C. Merriam, July 15, 1906, ibid. See also Nelson 1910; Broughton 1996.

35. Nels Nelson to J. C. Merriam, ibid.

36. Alfred L. Kroeber to Frederic W. Putnam, March 2, 1910, Putnam Papers.

37. Nels C. Nelson to John C. Merriam, June 15, 1907, Merriam Papers.

38. Nels Nelson to Pliny Goddard, April 24, 1911, Nels Nelson Papers.

39. MacCurdy, a friend of Osborn's, had been scheduled to arrange an exhibit of European Paleolithic materials at the AMNH. A letter from Goddard to Nelson, which mentions Wissler's interest in hiring "a certain old man of experience," appears to refer to MacCurdy. Clark Wissler to George G. MacCurdy, March 23, 1911, Correspondence files, Anthropology Archives, AMNH; Pliny Goddard to Nels Nelson, October 28, 1911, Nels Nelson Papers.

40. Pliny E. Goddard to Clark Wissler, September 28, 1911, Correspondence files, Anthropology Archives, AMNH.

41. Henry F. Osborn to Clark Wissler, June 1, 1911, Central Archives, AMNH; Nels Nelson to J. C. Merriam, July 22, 1911, Merriam Papers.

42. Francis W. Kelsey to Nels C. Nelson, March 4, 1911, Nels Nelson Papers.

43. Pliny E. Goddard to Clark Wissler, September 28, 1911, Correspondence files, Anthropology Archives, AMNH.

44. Nels C. Nelson to Pliny E. Goddard, November 29, 1911; Clark Wissler to Nels Nelson, December 12, 1911; both ibid.

45. Nelson married Kroeber's former secretary, Ethelyn Hobbs, in the spring of 1912. Nels Nelson to Clark Wissler, April 5, 1912, ibid.

46. A. V. Kidder to Pliny E. Goddard, January 24, 1912, ibid.

47. H. J. Spinden to Clark Wissler, September 14, 1909, Accession files 1910–57, Anthropology Archives, AMNH.

48. Nels Nelson to Pliny Goddard, September 8, 1912, Accession files 1912–52, Anthropology Archives, AMNH.

49. Clark Wissler to Nels Nelson, July 12, 1912, ibid.

50. Nels Nelson to Alfred A. Kroeber, August 26, 1912, Nels Nelson Papers.

51. Osborn 1918 [1915].

52. Nels Nelson to J. C. Merriam, March 21, 1913, Merriam Papers.

53. Nels C. Nelson to Clark Wissler, May 19, July 7, 1913, Correspondence files, Anthropology Archives, AMNH.

54. Nels Nelson to Clark Wissler, May 19, 1913, ibid.

55. Woodbury 1960a, 1960b.

56. Cabrera Valdés 1984: 31.

57. Nels C. Nelson to Alfred L. Kroeber, April 24, 1914, Nels Nelson Papers.

58. Nelson 1914.

59. Nels Nelson to Clark Wissler, November 26, 1914, Correspondence files, Anthropology Archives, AMNH.

60. Nelson 1916; Nels C. Nelson field journal, 1914, Nels Nelson Papers.

61. This point is made by Lyman et al 1997: 44.

62. Nelson 1916: 165.

63. Ibid.

64. A. V. Kidder was one of the first professionals to recognize Nelson's accomplishment, expressed in a note of praise written in February 1915. Alfred V. Kidder to Nels C. Nelson, February 16, 1915, Nels Nelson Papers.

65. Clark Wissler to Archer M. Huntington, January 28, 1915, Correspondence files, Anthropology Archives, AMNH.

66. Clark Wissler to Henry F. Osborn, June 30, 1914, Central Archives, AMNH.

67. Clark Wissler to Frederick A. Lucas, March 23, 1915, ibid.

68. Clark Wissler to A. E. Douglass, May 22, 1914; A. E. Douglass to Clark Wissler, June 5, 1914; both in Correspondence files, Anthropology Archives, AMNH.

69. Alfred L. Kroeber to Clark Wissler, February 11, 1915, ibid.

70. Alfred L. Kroeber to Clark Wissler, August 4, 1915, ibid.

71. Clark Wissler to Nels C. Nelson, August 23, 1915, ibid.

72. Clark Wissler to Alfred L. Kroeber, September 2, 1915, ibid.

73. Kroeber 1916.

74. Nels C. Nelson to Earl H. Morris, May 1, 1922, Nels Nelson Papers.

75. Nels C. Nelson to Sylvanus G. Morley, August 18, 1921, Correspondence files, Anthropology Archives, AMNH.
76. Clark Wissler to Sylvanus G. Morley, n.d. (summer 1921), Neil Merton Judd Papers, National Anthropological Archives, Smithsonian Institution.

References

Barton, D. R. 1941. "Mud, Stones, and History." *Natural History* 47 (5): 293–303.
Broughton, J. M., ed. 1996. *Excavation of the Emeryville Shellmound, 1906: Nels C. Nelson's Final Report*. Transcribed and prefaced by J. M. Broughton. Contributions of the University of California Archaeological Research Facility no. 54.
Browman, D. L. 2002. "Origins of Stratigraphic Excavations in North America: The Peabody Museum Method and the Chicago Method." In *New Perspectives on the Origins of Americanist Archaeology*, edited by D. L. Browman and S. Williams, 242–264. Tuscaloosa: University of Alabama Press.
Browman, D. L., and D. R. Givens. 1996. "Stratigraphic Excavation: The First 'New Archaeology.'" *American Anthropologist* 98 (1): 80–95.
Cabrera Valdés, V. 1984. *El Yacimiento de la Cueva de "El Castillo"* [The site of Castillo Cave]. Consejo Superior de Investigaciones Científicas, Instituto Español de Prehistoria, Madrid.
Freed, S. A., and R. S. Freed. 1983. "Clark Wissler and the Development of Anthropology in the United States." *American Anthropologist* 85 (4): 800–825.
———. 1992. "Clark Wissler." *Biographical Memoirs, National Academy of Sciences* 61: 469–496.
Kennedy, J. M. 1968. "Philanthropy and Science in New York City: The American Museum of Natural History, 1868–1968." Ph.D. diss., Yale University. Ann Arbor, Mich.: University Microfilms.
Kroeber, A. L. 1916. "Zuñi Potsherds." *American Museum of Natural History, Anthropological Papers* 18: 1–38.
Laufer, B. 1913. "Remarks on 'Some Aspects of North American Archaeology.'" *American Anthropologist* 15 (4): 573–577.
Lyman, R. L., M. J. O'Brien, and R. C. Dunnell. 1997. *The Rise and Fall of Culture History*. New York: Plenum.
Nelson, N. C. 1910. "The Ellis Landing Shellmound." *University of California Publications in Archaeology and Ethnology* 7 (5): 357–426.
———. 1914. "Pueblo Ruins of the Galisteo Basin, New Mexico." *American Museum of Natural History, Anthropological Papers* 15 (1): 1–124.
———. 1916. "Chronology of the Tano Ruins." *American Anthropologist* 18 (2): 159–180.
Osborn, H. F. 1915 [1918]. *Men of the Old Stone Age*. 3d ed. New York: Charles Scribner's Sons.

Praetzellis, A. 1993. "The Limits of Arbitrary Excavation." In *Practices of Archaeological Stratigraphy*, edited by E. C. Harris, M. R. Brown III, and G. J. Brown, 68–86. San Diego: Academic Press.

Proske, B. G. 1963. *Archer Milton Huntington*. New York: Hispanic Society of America.

Rainger, R. 1991. *An Agenda for Antiquity: Henry Fairfield Osborn and Vertebrate Paleontology at the American Museum of Natural History, 1890–1935*. Tuscaloosa: University of Alabama Press.

Rowe, J. H. 1954. "Max Uhle, 1856–1944: A Memoir of the Father of Peruvian Archaeology." *University of California Publications in American Archaeology and Ethnology* 46 (1).

Snead, J. E. 1999. "Science, Commerce, and Control: Patronage and the Development of Anthropological Archaeology in the Americas." *American Anthropologist* 101 (2): 256–271.

———. 2001. *Ruins and Rivals: The Making of Southwest Archaeology*. Tucson: University of Arizona Press.

Stock, C. 1938. "John Campbell Merriam as Scientist and Philosopher." In *Cooperation and Research by Staff Members and Research Associates: The Carnegie Institution of Washington*, 765–778. Carnegie Institute of Washington, Publication no. 501.

Wallace, W. J., and D. W. Lathrap. 1975. *West Berkeley (CA-ALA-307): A Culturally Stratified Shell Mound on the East Shore of San Francisco Bay*. Contributions of the University of California Archaeological Research Facility 29.

Willey, G. R., and J. A. Sabloff. 1993. *A History of American Archaeology*. 3d ed. London: Thames and Hudson.

Woodbury, R. B. 1960a. "Nels C. Nelson and Chronological Archaeology." *American Antiquity* 25: 400–401.

———. 1960b. "Nelson's Stratigraphy." *American Antiquity* 26: 98–99.

5

Nels Nelson and the Measure of Time

Michael J. O'Brien

Nels Nelson was born in Denmark in 1875 and immigrated to the United States in 1892. He eventually found his way to the University of California and became a student of A. L. Kroeber, who had recently completed his doctorate under Franz Boas at Columbia University and moved west to build the Anthropology Department at Berkeley. By 1906, Nelson had become involved in an ongoing investigation of shell mounds along San Francisco Bay being directed by paleontologist John C. Merriam, working at two of them, Ellis Landing (Nelson 1910) and Emeryville (Nelson [1906] 1996). The latter midden had been explored earlier in the decade by Friedrich Max Uhle, a German archaeologist employed by the University of California, who reported his findings at Emeryville in terms of culture change over time (Uhle 1907). As has been well documented in histories of Americanist archaeology (e.g., Lyman et al. 1997; Willey and Sabloff 1993), Uhle's findings did not impress Kroeber, who controlled the funding for university-sponsored archaeology. In a general review of California archaeology that he prepared for a volume honoring Harvard prehistorian Frederic Ward Putnam, Kroeber (1909) criticized Uhle (without naming him) for his interpretations of culture change in the San Francisco Bay area. To Kroeber, who at the time believed that the presence of humans in North America was on the order of a couple thousand years at best, there had not been any significant change from the bottom through the top of the Emeryville Shell Mound. When Nelson wrote the report on Ellis Landing (Nelson 1910), he took a much more conservative approach than Uhle had.

It might seem odd to begin a discussion of Nels Nelson with a recounting of the work of another person and the criticism it engendered, but it is impossible to understand the place Nelson's work assumed in early-twentieth-century Americanist archaeology without raising two issues —stratigraphic excavation and chronology—and Kroeber's reaction to Uhle's work is the perfect vehicle for doing that. Without this background, brief though it is, Nelson's real contribution to Americanist archaeology becomes entangled in arguments over the origins of stratigraphic excavation. Nelson has long been credited with "revolutionizing" Americanist archaeology by being one of the first, if not the first, to recognize that recovering artifacts by stratigraphic level allowed one to measure the passage of time (Adams 1960; Browman and Givens 1996; Heizer 1959; Meera 1940; Taylor 1954; Woodbury 1960a, 1960b). It was not his work in California to which these and other authors were referring, but rather his work in the Galisteo Basin of New Mexico a few years later. Robert Heizer (1959: 216) went so far as to state that "N. C. Nelson's [1916] summary of his Tano excavations marks the beginning of a new era in American archaeology, since it called attention effectively to the results which stratigraphic excavation could produce." This was a significant misstatement on Heizer's part, but it sums up the general sentiment of the discipline as to the origins of stratigraphic excavation in North America and the person responsible for its introduction from Europe.

This sentiment, however, overlooks the fact that prehistorians had made observations based on stratigraphic positioning of artifacts, the "results" that Heizer mentioned, long before Nelson started working in New Mexico. Nelson himself had done it at Ellis Landing, and Uhle had done it several years earlier at Emeryville. The problem in determining the origin of stratigraphic excavation in North America rests on how one defines "excavating stratigraphically." Some historians of archaeology (e.g., Browman and Givens 1996) define it conservatively, meaning that for an exercise to qualify, an archaeologist has to excavate in levels, be they natural or artificial, and segregate artifacts according to those levels. Others (e.g., Lyman and O'Brien 1999; O'Brien and Lyman 1999) define it more liberally, focusing more on how materials are removed and segregated than on whether excavation is undertaken. After all, the law of superposition, which says that things at the bottom of a vertical sequence were deposited before things at the top, holds true regardless of whether one actually moves sediment to secure a stratigraphic section (e.g., Dall 1877; Harrington 1909; Peabody 1904, 1908, 1910; Peabody and Moorehead 1904; Pepper 1920 [working in 1896–99]; Will and Spinden 1906) or uses natural cuts (e.g., Holmes 1885; Pepper 1916 [working in 1904]; Schrabisch 1909) from which to make stratigraphic observations. Even using the more conservative definition, the references above, and there are literally dozens more (Lyman and O'Brien 1999), demonstrate that North American prehistorians before Nelson were excavating stratigraphically.

Perhaps historians of archaeology have been led astray by the words not of someone disconnected to Nelson and his work but of someone who knew Nelson's work intimately. That someone was Leslie Spier, who was a colleague of Nelson when they worked for the American Museum of Natural History in New York. In a retrospective look at Nelson's work, Spier (1931: 275) stated that Nelson's use of superposition (in New Mexico) was "the first exposition of a refined method for determining exactly the time sequence of archaeological materials in a primitive area." Was Spier, who was in a position to know, saying there was something distinctive and revolutionary about *how* Nelson excavated? No. Although Nelson was deliberate in his method of excavation—laying out units and working in precise levels—he was not the first Americanist to work in such a manner (e.g., Peabody and Moorehead 1904). The revolutionary aspect of Nelson's work to which Spier was referring had to do with how Nelson analyzed archaeological materials derived from the excavation units. This was a most remarkable accomplishment and one that has gone unappreciated in the archaeological literature. In the following section, I outline both the archaeological problems that Nelson set out to solve and the methods he used to solve them.

Nelson in the Galisteo Basin

Nelson left San Francisco after completing his master's degree and was hired by Clark Wissler of the American Museum to begin a field project in the Galisteo Basin, just south of Santa Fe, New Mexico. The basin contained a large number of Puebloan ruins, and it was on these that Wissler and Nelson turned their collective attention in 1911. In a popular article titled "Ruins of Prehistoric New Mexico" that he published in the *American Museum Journal,* Nelson explained why he was in the Southwest in the first place:

It is felt that many problems relating to the origin and distribution of peoples and to cultural traits now observable in the Southwest cannot be solved in their entirety by the examination of present-day conditions or even by consulting Spanish documentary history, which though it takes us back nearly four hundred years and is reasonably accurate, shows us little more than the last phase of development within this most interesting ethnographic division of the United States. By a tolerably exhaustive study of the thousands of ruins and other archaeological features characteristic of the region, we may hope in time to gain not only an idea of prehistoric conditions but perhaps also an adequate explanation of the origin, the antiquity and the course of development leading up to a better understanding of the present status of aboriginal life in the region. (Nelson 1913: 63)

Wissler indicated that the "plan was to take up the historical problem in the Southwest to determine if possible the relations between the prehistoric and historic peoples" (1915: 395). Toward that end, the area chosen, apparently by Wissler, was what "seemed most likely to have been the chief center of Pueblo culture as we now know it" (ibid.: 397).

The above quotation from Nelson's 1913 paper is important for several reasons, not the least of which is the damage it does to statements that Nelson revolutionized Americanist archaeology by excavating stratigraphically in the Galisteo Basin, especially at the site of San Cristóbal in 1914–15. If such statements are true, then we are led to believe that Nelson was unaware of the chronological significance of superposed artifacts prior to his work in the Galisteo Basin. If so, then how was he supposed to explain "the antiquity and the course of development" of prehistoric peoples there? Did Wissler send Nelson off on a wild goose chase, only to have Nelson, through a stroke of genius, stumble upon the importance of superposed artifacts for marking the passage of time? The answer is decidedly no; Nelson, Wissler, Spier, and almost any other Americanist archaeologist at that time, knew the value of superposed artifacts, and some of them suspected there was much deeper antiquity to the human presence in North America than was commonly appreciated.

The issue of human antiquity was debated throughout the late nineteenth century, and the opinion was badly split. On the side favoring considerable antiquity was Putnam and those he either employed or influenced from his position at the Peabody Museum (Harvard). The group included prehistorians such as Thomas Wilson of the U.S. National Museum and Warren Moorehead of the Phillips Academy in Andover, Massachusetts; geologists such as Henry Lewis and G. Frederick Wright; and paleontologists/geologists such as Henry W. Haynes. Their arguments in favor of a great antiquity for humans on the continent, an antiquity that extended back to at least the end of the Pleistocene, were based not only on the stratigraphic position of presumed artifacts in glacial deposits but also on the similarities between Paleolithic tools in the Old World and the rather crude tools found in various North American gravel deposits, including the most publicized of all, the Trenton gravels in New Jersey (Holmes 1893b; Spier 1916; Volk 1911; Wissler 1916). Proponents argued that since the two sets of tools looked the same, they must date to the same time period (e.g., Wilson 1889, 1895).

The faulty logic behind this argument was not lost on those on the opposite side of the issue, primarily members of the Bureau of American Ethnology (BAE) in Washington, D.C. Chief among them was William Henry Holmes, who began as early as 1890 with a series of articles aimed at discrediting the great antiquity of humans in the New World (e.g., Holmes 1892, 1893a, 1893b, 1897a, 1897b). Part of his strategy was to demonstrate the stages of manufacture that stone implements went through and thereby show that items others had bandied about as ancient implements were instead preforms or quarry rejects of comparatively recent age. This led to his excavations in quarries in the Washington, D.C., area and finally to his article titled "Stone Implements of the Potomac–Chesapeake Tidewater Province," published in the *Fifteenth Annual Report, Bureau of Ethnology, 1893–1894* (Holmes 1897b). In it Holmes conclusively demonstrated (1) the universal reduction process that raw stone goes through on its way to being a finished piece, and (2) the similarity in form between rejects and blanks in American quarries and Paleolithic implements from Europe. The take-home message was clear: Do not confuse crude American quarry waste and "blanks" with finished implements, even though the waste or "blanks" resemble true European Paleolithic tools.

Most histories of archaeology, in treating the issue of an American Paleolithic, concentrate on what was said during the debate and ignore the underlying reasons for the rift that developed in American archaeology over the question of human antiquity. David Meltzer (1983, 1985, 1991), in an excellent analysis of the period, points out that the fundamental issue was in the way that BAE archaeologists viewed the past as opposed to how archaeologists working outside the bureau viewed it. Bureau personnel saw the North American archaeological record as essentially one that had been left by the Indians and not by an unrelated group of mound builders that had preceded them. The BAE's strategy from the start had been to use archaeology to extend back in time the story of the American Indian, and that story certainly did not need "the idea of an earlier, unrelated Paleolithic 'race'" (Meltzer and Dunnell 1992: xxxiii). Non-BAE prehistorians, however, did not share this atemporal view, and it was they who argued vehemently that the gravel beds contained rich in situ deposits of Paleolithic tools. Nelson would later have something to say about Pleistocene-age humans in North America (Nelson 1928a, 1928b), but neither he nor Kroeber played an active role in the arguments at the turn of the century. Ironically, it would be a locale just to the northeast of the Galisteo Basin that would produce convincing evidence of humans in association with late Pleistocene-age fauna (Figgins 1927), but at the time Nelson began working in New Mexico the majority of prehistorians assumed that human tenure in North America was on the order of a few thousand years at the most. Kroeber certainly was one of these. He was echoing the words of his mentor, Boas (1902), when he pointed out that with respect to the culture history of the Americas, the

> civilization revealed by [archaeology] is in its essentials the same as that found in the same region by the more recent explorer and settler. . . . Neither archaeology nor ethnology has yet been able to discover either the presence or absence of any important cultural features in one period that are not respectively present or absent in the other . . . [and] archaeology at no point gives any evidence of significant changes in culture. . . . Differences between the past and present are only differences in detail, involving nothing more than a *passing change of fashion* in manufacture or in manipulation of the same process. (Kroeber 1909: 3–5; emphasis added)

John Rowe (1962: 399–400) argued that in 1909 Kroeber was visualizing "cultural change in terms of major shifts in technology and subsistence, any changes of less moment [such as what Uhle documented] were insignificant." Uhle seems to have favored a gradualistic form of cultural evolution, whereas Kroeber favored a punctuated form such as that represented by Europe's Paleolithic–Neolithic–Bronze Age–Iron Age sequence, in which change through time was marked by major differences in materials. Kroeber, like Boas, knew full well the value of data regarding the stratigraphic context of artifacts; such data were an "urgent need" if one was to acquire "information as to cultural and chronological relations" (Kroeber 1909: 39, 41). Thus, he did not discount the *value* of Uhle's stratigraphic method; rather, he questioned the significance of the *chronological indications* of cultural change Uhle documented. There were few artifacts; they showed no marked cultural changes; change was in "quality and finish . . . rather than [in the introduction of] new types"; and "the principal types . . . occur in all strata" (Kroeber 1923: 141). For Kroeber

(1909: 15), these observations indicated the "same modes of life . . . were followed in the periods represented by the earliest and the lat st strata." Any change was, as pointed out in the quotation above, mere y "a passing change of fashion in manufacture or in manipulation of the s me process" and not "to be compared even for a moment with a transi on as fundamental as that from palaeolithic to neolithic" (Kroeber 190?: 16).

This was the line of reasoning held by almost all Americanists in the early decades of the twentieth century, regardless of how they read the evidence for or against a long human record on the continent. Change, to be significant, had to be epochal in nature. Rowe (1962) was correct: anything less than major shifts in technology and subsistence were inconsequential. Putnam and others thought they saw such change, and they used it as evidence of deep antiquity. Holmes, Kroeber, and others did not see large discontinuities in the archaeological record and relegated the small changes they *did* see to a mere "passing change of fashion" (Kroeber 1909: 5). It was this mind-set that Nelson inherited, which makes what he did all the more remarkable in that he transcended his intellectual heritage and showed how to construct a chronometer that measured time continuously as opposed to discontinuously.

In his report on the work at Ellis Landing, Nelson, being well aware of Kroeber's (1909) recent salvo across Uhle's (1907) bow, did not address chronological issues, despite his estimate that the shell mound had formed over some 3,500 years (Nelson 1910: 371). But he *did* address chronological issues in the Galisteo Basin. In a critical passage from his final report, "Chronology of the Tano Ruins, New Mexico," which was published in *American Anthropologist,* Nelson noted,

> The greater portion of the country in question seems unfit for almost any sort of aboriginal existence, being either mountainous or desertlike plateau, lacking water. . . . [Yet] there are on record for the region about three hundred [prehistoric] ruins, some of them very large. [A complete survey would probably] reveal twice the listed number of abandoned pueblos. . . . [Thus,] the implied population mounts to figures out of proportion on the one hand, to the productivity of the country and on the other, to the historically known facts. We may, therefore, reasonably suspect a lengthy occupation by either a shifting or a changing population; in other words, that the ruins in question *are not of the same age* (1916: 161; emphasis added).

In other words, Nelson figured there *had* to be temporal difference in order to account for all those people who had occupied all those sites—a conclusion reached concurrently by Nelson's museum colleague Spier, who was then working in New Jersey. After completing a survey in 1912, Spier (1913: 677) noted that "the number of sites within [the] limited area [examined] is too large for all to have belonged to [the historical] period." Nelson's objective in New Mexico, similar to Spier's in New Jersey, was to demonstrate that a chronological span, and perhaps a lengthy one, was present in the middens and roof fall of the Galisteo pueblos. He did so in revolutionary fashion not by excavating stratigraphically but by arranging the frequencies of pottery types, or styles, against their vertical provenience and inferring that the shifting frequencies marked the passage of time (Nelson 1916).

In his report, Nelson (1916) stated that by the beginning of the 1914 season he suspected he knew the chronological order of five types of pottery, two of which exhibited painted designs and three of which contained glazed designs. He pointed out that in some cases the glaze was of a "consistency halfway between glaze and paint," but he emphasized that in other cases it was a "genuinely *vitrified* coating, resisting a knife point, and every bit equal to the glaze on modern crockery" (1916: 173). One of the painted types was suspected of being the earliest of the five, occurring as it did on numerous small, suspected pre-Puebloan sites in northern New Mexico. The other painted type was known to be the latest of the five types because it occurred in abundance on sites historically documented as postdating the Pueblo Revolt of 1680. Nelson viewed one of the three glazed types as being from the early historical period (1540–1680), given that it was found consistently with bones of horses and other historically introduced domestic animals. The other two glazed types were slid in between the early painted type and the historical-period glazed type. Despite his intuitions regarding the chronological arrangement of the types, he (1916: 162) noted that "tangible proof was still wanting."

Nelson tested the suspected sequence of types first at Paako, a ruin just northeast of Albuquerque, and then late in the 1914 field season at Pueblo San Cristóbal in the Galisteo Basin. He followed up that work the next year with excavations at three other pueblos, San Marcos, Cieneguilla, and Arroyo Hondo. Nelson excavated San Cristóbal (and presumably the other sites) in arbitrary 1-foot-thick levels (fig. 5.1) rather than in natural stratigraphic units, and he kept sherds from each level separate and identified and counted them by level. This is the feature of his work that has

Fig. 5.1. Stratigraphic cut made by Nels Nelson through midden deposit at San Cristóbal, New Mexico. From Nelson 1916 (courtesy American Museum of Natural History).

Fig. 5.2. *Left to right:* Nels Nelson, Abbé Henri Breuil, Hugo Obermaier, Paul Wernert, and Pierre Teilhard de Chardin at Castillo Cave, Spain, 1913. Photograph by M. C. Burkitt, negative no. 124770 (courtesy Department of Library Services, American Museum of Natural History).

received attention in histories of Americanist archaeology. Nelson had visited the stratigraphic excavations of Otto Obermaier and Henri Breuil in Spain in 1913 (fig. 5.2) and had seen "levels marked off on the walls" of the excavations, and he had participated in excavating Castillo Cave— an experience that, according to Nelson (Woodbury 1960b: 98), served as "chief inspiration" for his excavation method at San Cristóbal. His technique of excavating in arbitrary levels might have come from Europe, but certainly not the notion that superposed collections marked the passage of time. Everyone knew that; the only debate was over *how* much time was being measured.

Nelson might have been impressed by what he saw Obermaier, Breuil, and others doing in Europe, but he ran into immediate problems in the Galisteo Basin, and the way he overcame them showed considerable insight. As he described the situation (1916), the problem was twofold. First, it was difficult to find unmixed deposits. Site-formation processes— excavation of burial pits, construction of house walls, and the like by the inhabitants of the sites—had jumbled the archaeological deposits, making it next to impossible to find clean stratigraphic sections. Second, when he *was* able to find undisturbed contexts, the pottery sequences were broken. None of the sites exhibited a complete sequence from the early painted type on the bottom up through the late painted type of the historical period. Further, in those places where he found evidence of chronological differentiation, it usually was only at the ends of a continuum of several pottery types. Thus he lamented that such instances were "merely clean-cut superpositions showing nothing but time relations" (Nelson 1916: 163). What he wanted was types in the continuum that were found stratigraphically mixed together, "one gradually replacing the other[. This] accounted for the otherwise unknown time that separated the merely superposed occurrences of types and from the point of view of the merely physical relationships of contiguity, connected them" (ibid.). In other words, instead of a stratigraphic column that showed "merely superposed occurrences of types," he wanted vertical overlap among types. He found such overlap at Pueblo San Marcos and Pueblo Arroyo Hondo, where "the ancient type of glazed ware twice noticed [at other sites] in contact with the [early] black-on-white [painted] ware was found actually mixed with it, the one gradually replacing the other" (ibid.). He later found the same kind of overlap, but of more types, at San Cristóbal.

The importance of overlap strongly suggests that Nelson was replacing the then-prevalent notion, founded in Lewis Henry Morgan's (1877) view of cultural evolution and shown most clearly in Kroeber's views, that culture change could be modeled as a flight of stairs, with each step representing a static evolutionary stage, or epochal event, and each riser a rather abrupt transformation from one stage to the next, with a model that viewed culture change as a gradually ascending ramp (Nelson 1919a, 1919b, 1932), albeit a ramp that moved through progressively more advanced stages (Lyman and O'Brien 1997). Plotting frequencies of types against time (rendered as geologically vertical space) would illustrate the gradual and continuous cultural evolution Nelson sought and eventually allow one to document the relative ages of the cultural stages (e.g., Nelson 1937).

Table 5.1 shows the absolute frequencies of the three types of pottery that Nelson recovered from his master stratigraphic column at San Cristóbal, which he claimed was excavated "with my own hands" (Nelson 1916: 165). Types IV and V, from the historical period, did not occur in the column. Figure 5.3 illustrates four of the pottery types (the late painted type is not included). Nelson obviously relied primarily on surface treatment as the basis for creating the types, and he referred to them in terms

Table 5.1. Frequencies of sherds by type and level in Nelson's stratigraphic column at San Cristóbal, New Mexico

Thickness of section		Corrugated ware	Biscuit ware	Black-on-white painted ware	Type I, 2- and 3-color painted ware	Type II, 2-color glazed ware		Type III, 3-color glazed ware
					black or brown glaze design	Red ware, Yellow ware, black or brown glaze	Gray ware, black or brown glaze	Gray, yellow, pink, and reddish wares, combination glaze-and-paint
		(1)	(2)	(3)	(4)	(5)	(6)	(7)
1st	ft	57	10	2	24	23	34	5
2d	"	116	17	2	64	90	76	6
3d	"	27	2	10	68	18	48	3
4th	"	28	4	6	52	20	21	
5th	"	60	15	2	128	55	85	
6th	"	75	21	8	192	53	52	1?
7th	"	53	10	40	91	20	15	
8th	"	56	2	118	45	1	5	
9th	"	93	1?	107	3			
10th	"	84	1?	69				
= 8 in.ᵃ		(126)		(103)				

a. Apparently, only 8 inches of the 11th foot were excavated, and the sherd counts were put in parentheses because they were from only part of a 1-ft. section.

of those treatments. Type I was referred to as "two- and three-color painted ware," type II as "two-color glazed ware," type III as "three-color glazed ware," type IV as "historic two-color glazed ware," and type V as "modern painted pottery." Along with the five wares that he actually referred to as "types" (I–V) were two other wares. One he termed "biscuit ware," calling it a "peculiar kind of pottery, which can be detected even by the touch," and another "corrugated or coiled ware," which "is almost invariably covered with soot and was evidently made exclusively for cooking purposes" (Nelson 1916: 168).

Notice that in his categorization, Nelson made use of several dimensions of variation. One dimension, the number of colors painted on a vessel, had to do with decoration; another, biscuit ware and corrugated ware, had to do with the initial stage of vessel manufacturing; and a third, the presence of glazing, although decorative, could also be technological in that glaze seals the vessel surface, thereby making it impermeable. Although Nelson mixed and matched decorative and what might be termed "technofunctional" vessel characters, the resulting types formed fairly homogeneous groups, meaning that vessels and sherds within any one type bore more resemblance to each other than they did to specimens in other types. Could he have constructed different types using the same pottery assemblages? Yes, and in fact Nelson (1916: 168) freely admitted that his classification was "no doubt arbitrary, but it will serve present purposes." The classification did indeed serve "present purposes," which was to establish a way to measure time and thereby produce a chronological ordering of archaeological materials in the north-central Rio Grande region of New Mexico, and it did it very well.

In presenting the absolute abundances of each of his five types of pottery from each of his 10 levels at San Cristóbal (table 5.1), Nelson in two instances adjusted some observed sherd frequencies to account for different excavation volumes—a rather innovative procedure for the time. His adjustment of observed frequencies, however, is unnecessary if the relative, or proportional, abundances of the artifacts are calculated—standard practice in modern archaeology. A. V. Kidder, who was working at Pecos Pueblo just to the east of where Nelson was working, also presumed that different excavation volumes compromised the usefulness of artifact-frequency data, noting with regard to using strata as artifact-collection units that the method "derogates from the absolute statistical value of the material, as the cuts, not being of exactly equal thickness, are not strictly comparable statistically" (Kidder and Kidder 1917: 340). It is unclear why Nelson and Kidder assumed that type frequencies must be adjusted to

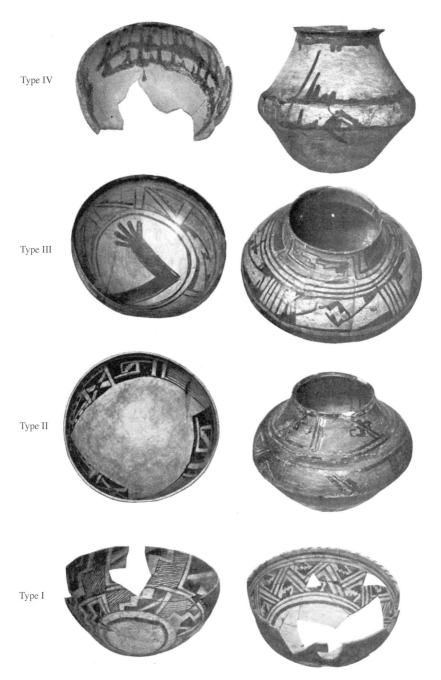

Type IV

Type III

Type II

Type I

Fig. 5.3. Four types of pottery constructed by Nels Nelson based on his excavations in the Galisteo Basin of New Mexico. From Nelson 1916 (courtesy of the American Museum of Natural History).

account for different excavation volumes. Maybe they were attempting to make the clearly relative time scale of superposition more absolute, as implied in Kroeber's (1919: 259) assessment of Nelson's excavation: "Each foot of debris may be taken as representing an approximately equal duration of deposition, as indicated by the fairly steady number of sherds of all types found at each depth." Rates of pottery deposition would influence absolute abundances of sherds, but only if the rate of sediment deposition remained constant throughout the sequence.

The important innovation found in Nelson's work is his demonstration that pottery types altered in absolute frequency through time in a pattern that he characterized as "very nearly normal frequency curves [that reflected the fact that] a style of pottery . . . came slowly into vogue, attained a maximum and began a gradual decline" (Nelson 1916: 167). Elsewhere, Lyman and I (Lyman and O'Brien 1999; Lyman et al. 1997, 1998; O'Brien and Lyman 1999) refer to this as the *popularity principle*. Figure 5.4 shows Nelson's data graphically as percentages of four pottery types by excavation level. Three of his types are of particular chronological usefulness in that they have continuous distributions in time. Note that corrugated ware does not pass what Alex Krieger (1944) referred to as the "historical-significance test," but types I–III do. Passing the historical-significance test means the types have "demonstrable historical meaning" (Krieger 1944: 272): they come into being, gain in popularity to a maximum, and then begin to fade, finally disappearing. Corrugated ware does not do this. Once it comes in (at a point in time older than the sequence shown), it persists alongside all other types. Biscuit ware is more difficult to judge (table 5.1), but it too "runs a rather unsteady course from beginning to end" (Nelson 1916: 166), making it useless as a historical type. Chronologically useful types can not "reappear" at a later date, which is more or less what biscuit ware does between the fifth and second levels at San Cristóbal (table 5.1). In terms of what Nelson was attempting to do, time's arrow, not time's cycle, is of interest (Lyman and O'Brien 1999), which is not to say the latter will not be of interest given an analytical problem other than marking the passage of time, such as examining adaptive features. When we plot the relative frequency of a good historical type through time, we should obtain a reasonably close approximation of a normal (unimodal) curve. If we get a discontinuous distribution or a multimodal curve over time, then the type as constructed is useless for chronological purposes.

By using the three types he did (Types I–III in table 5.1), Nelson was able to measure culture change using not the then-typical qualitative dif-

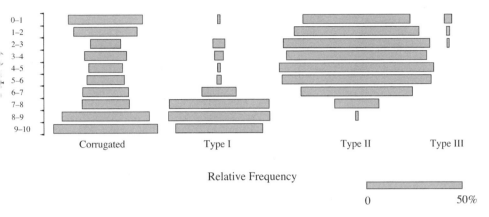

Fig. 5.4. Nels Nelson's pottery data from Pueblo San Cristóbal, New Mexico, showing the waxing and waning popularity of types. Note that Nelson believed, correctly, that the frequency of corrugated ware was not a good indicator of age. Note also the essentially monotonic frequency distribution of his types I–III. Data from Nelson 1916.

ferences in artifact assemblages such as the presence or absence of pottery, as had been done by numerous prehistorians up to that point, or by plotting frequencies of technological and functional types of artifacts against their vertical recovery proveniences, such as he had done earlier with materials from sites along San Francisco Bay (Nelson 1906, 1910). Rather, he detected culture change and thus the passage of time by documenting, in revolutionary fashion, the changing frequencies of pottery *types,* or *styles* (Lyman and O'Brien 2000). Did Nelson simply get lucky in that his types measured time? If he had created other types instead of the ones he did, would they also have been good chronological types? Maybe, but the point is that the ones he *did* create were not simply the products of luck. They were based on observations, both stratigraphic and otherwise, that Nelson and others made in the Pueblo region of New Mexico. Might someone argue that it is tautological to use stratigraphic observations to construct types that then will be used to measure the passage of time? If Nelson or someone else had never tested his types to determine their chronological reliability outside the site where the stratigraphic observations were made, then that would be not only tautological but also bad science. But Nelson *did* check the sequence of types. It is clear that his celebrated work at San Cristóbal was simply a confirmatory exercise, not a creational one, despite how it has since been perceived.

Nelson could have ended his discussion with his stratigraphic observations, but he took them a step further:

Accepting the foregoing chronological deduction as essentially correct, we may properly conclude this study by trying out our scheme on some of the ruins in the territory to which it applies. A limited amount of data in the way of potsherds, etc., is available for several subdivisions of the glazed pottery area and judging from these it seems probable that the entire region underwent about the same stylistic changes. But for present purposes it will be enough to illustrate the possibilities of chronological determination by applying the facts at hand to the Tano district from which alone our data are nearly complete. Substituting for the five successive pottery types a corresponding number of time periods we get the following results, set forth in tabular form. (Nelson 1916: 178, 180)

Nelson's tabular form is reproduced in table 5.2. He noted that there was a trend toward a decreasing number of sites through time, although he remarked that this should not be taken as a population decrease because his impression was that "as the villages decreased in number they increased in size" (Nelson 1916: 180). In essence, Nelson took the first step toward creating an occurrence-seriation graph, although he did not take the second step and arrange the sites in chronological order. It is apparent from the graph that several sites either contained sherds from all five "periods" (San Marcos) or possibly contained them (San Cristóbal, San Lazaro, Galisteo, and San Pedro Viejo [marked by question marks]), but as Nelson pointed out, no single stratigraphic section contained sherds of all five periods. Thus he pieced together, or "interdigitated" (Lyman et al. 1998; O'Brien and Lyman 1998), several sections to obtain the complete sequence.

Conclusion

From this brief discussion it should be clear that the so-called stratigraphic revolution in Americanist archaeology did not reside in a change in excavation technique. Rather, it resided in a shift in how variation in artifacts was measured—a shift that made culture change and thus time visible. As Nelson (1919a: 134) observed a few years after what we might most accurately call the "historical-type revolution," the research of Kidder, Kroeber, Spier, and Nelson himself indicated that pottery was "the most readily available single trait through which to trace the preliminary outlines of Pueblo history." Nelson (1919a: 134) noted that "ceramics, or pottery," worked well for measuring time "mainly because of its variability." He elaborated that "utilitarian objects," or what we today would term functional classes, "would not serve because they are much the same the world over," whereas with respect "to both form and decoration, [pottery] gives infinite opportunity for the expression of individual taste and talent and the resulting differentiation in the product from place to place and from time to time is the key to the [chronological] problem." True, but Nelson could have added that it was the ability to use changes in frequency of multiple pottery types that was the *real* key to the chronological problem. What he accomplished was possible only because of how he viewed culture change—not in terms of epochal events but as a continuum. Note how he ended his 1916 report:

When the very considerable quantities of crushed pottery vessels obtained during three seasons of excavation have been assembled . . . it should be possible to observe either a series of sharp breaks in the symbolism on the pottery, or else a gradual development of motifs. Such a study it now seems probable will show that the successive styles of ceramics arose the one from the other and that therefore, by inference, we may assume a relatively steady and uneventful career for the people inhabiting the Tano territory.

As important as Nelson's insights were, the discipline at large never widely adopted the notion of continuous change. Once the Pecos Classification caught hold in the Southwest and archaeologists began thinking in terms of periods and the like, the model of culture change that guided Nelson's work was replaced wholesale with a model that emphasized cultures as static entities. Change, then, was rendered as a series of cultural replacements—the epochal events emphasized by Kroeber and others. The pottery types that Nelson had used to measure the "relatively steady and uneventful career" of prehistoric peoples were co-opted as index markers that could be used to identify various prehistoric cultures. Stratigraphic excavation provided those markers, and Nelson was identified as the person responsible for introducing the notion of superposition to Americanist archaeology. In the process, the truly revolutionary aspect of his work was completely overlooked.

Table 5.2. Periods represented by sherds from pueblos in the Tano District, New Mexico

No.	Name of locality		Pre-pueblo period	Pueblo periods			IV (1540–1680)	V (1680 on)	No. of rooms excavated
				I	II	III			
1	White Rock Cañon,	No. 1		X	X				
2	" "	" 2		X	X				
3	Boom Camp			X	X				
4	Los Aguajes				X	X			33 +
5	Santa Fé			X					
6	Agua Fria,	No. 1		X	X				
7	" "	" 2		X	X				
8	Cieneguilla			X	X	X		X	132
9	Cienega,	No. 1		X				X	
10	"	" 2							
11	"	" 3		X	X				45
12	"	" 4	X						Trenched
13	La Bajada,	No. 1		X	X				
14	" "	" 2			X	X			84+
15	Canyoncito,	No. 1			?	X			9+
16	"	" 2				X			
17	"	" 3		X					
18	"	" 4	X						
19	Arroyo Hondo,	No. 1		X					
20	"	" 2		X	X				12
21	Peñas Negras			X					108+

No.	Site								Count
22	Chamisalocita Cañon			X						44+
23	Alamo Cañon			X						27+
24	Mansanaria,			X						Trenched
25	"	" 1		X						5+
26	Lamy	" 1		X						
27	"	" 2		X						2
28	"	" 3		X						17
29	San Marcos			X	X	X	X		X	172+
30	Cañon Casita			X	X		X		?	
31	San Cristobal			X	X	X	X			239+
32	Largo				X	X	X			13+
33	Colorado				X	X	X			47+
34	Shé				X	X	X			28+
35	Blanco				X	X	X			47+
36	San Lazaro				X	X	X	X	?	60+
37	Galisteo				X	X	X		?	25+
38	Gipuy (Old Domingo)					X	X			
39	Ojito Juan Pedro				X	X	X			
40	Pinavetitas Cañon					X	X			
41	San Pedro Viej (2)		(X)	X	X	X	X	X	?	174+
42	Uña de Gato,	No. 1		X		?				
43	" " "	" 2			X	X	X			
44	Tunque					X	X	X		239+
45	Algodones		X				X			
	Totals		4	29	21	19	6	3		1562

Acknowledgments

I thank Jim Truncer for his invitation to contribute to this volume. Most of the ideas expressed in this paper are as much Lee Lyman's as they are mine.

References

Adams, R. E. 1960. "Manual Gamio and Stratigraphic Excavation." *American Antiquity* 26: 99.
Boas, F. 1902. "Some Problems in North American Archaeology." *American Journal of Archaeology* 6: 1–6.
Browman, D. L., and D. R. Givens. 1996. "Stratigraphic Excavation: The First 'New Archaeology.'" *American Anthropologist* 98: 80–95.
Dall, W. H. 1877. "On Succession in the Shell-Heaps of the Aleutian Islands." *Contributions to North American Ethnology* 1: 41–91.
Figgins, J. D. 1927. "The Antiquity of Man in America." *Natural History* 27: 229–239.
Harrington, M. R. 1909. "The Rock-Shelters of Armonk, New York." In *The Indians of Greater New York and the Lower Hudson*, edited by C. Wissler. *American Museum of Natural History, Anthropological Papers* 3: 123–138.
Heizer, R. F. 1959. *The Archaeologist at Work: A Source Book in Archaeological Method and Interpretation*. New York: Harper.
Holmes, W. H. 1885. "Evidences of the Antiquity of Man on the Site of the City of Mexico." *Anthropological Society of Washington, Transactions* 3: 68–81.
———. 1892. "Modern Quarry Refuse and the Paleolithic Theory." *Science* 20: 295–297.
———. 1893a. "Distribution of Stone Implements in the Tidewater Country." *American Anthropologist* 6: 1–14.
———. 1893b. "Are There Traces of Man in the Trenton Gravels?" *Journal of Geology* 1: 15–37.
———. 1897a. "Primitive Man in the Delaware Valley." *Science* 26: 824–829.
———. 1897b. "Stone Implements of the Potomac–Chesapeake Tidewater Province." *Fifteenth Annual Report, Bureau of Ethnology, 1893–1894*, 13–152. Washington, D.C.: Government Printing Office.
Kidder, M. A., and A. V. Kidder. 1917. "Notes on the Pottery of Pecos." *American Anthropologist* 19: 325–360.
Krieger, A. D. 1944. "The Typological Concept." *American Antiquity* 9: 271–288.
Kroeber, A. L. 1909. "The Archaeology of California." In *Putnam Anniversary Volume*, edited by F. Boas, 1–42. New York: Stechert.
———. 1919. "On the Principle of Order in Civilization as Exemplified by Changes of Fashion." *American Anthropologist* 21: 235–263.

———. 1923. "The History of Native Culture in California." *University of California, Publications in American Archaeology and Ethnology* 20: 123–142.

Lyman, R. L., and M. J. O'Brien. 1997. "The Concept of Evolution in Early Twentieth-Century Americanist Archaeology." In *Rediscovering Darwin: Evolutionary Theory in Archeological Explanation*, edited by C. M. Barton and G. A. Clark, 21–48. *American Anthropological Association, Archeological Papers* No. 7. Washington, D.C.

———. 1999. "Americanist Stratigraphic Excavation and the Measurement of Culture Change." *Journal of Archaeological Method and Theory* 6: 55–108.

———. 2000. "Chronometers and Units in Early Archaeology and Paleontology." *American Antiquity* 65: 691–707.

Lyman, R. L., M. J. O'Brien, and R. C. Dunnell. 1997. *The Rise and Fall of Culture History.* New York: Plenum.

Lyman, R. L., S. Wolverton, and M. J. O'Brien. 1998. "Seriation, Superposition, and Interdigitation: A History of Americanist Graphic Depictions of Culture Change." *American Antiquity* 63: 239–261.

Meera, H. P. 1940. "Ceramic Clues to the Prehistory of North Central New Mexico." Laboratory of Anthropology, Technical Series Bulletin No. 8. Santa Fe, N.M.

Meltzer, D. J. 1983. "The Antiquity of Man and the Development of American Archaeology." In *Advances in Archaeological Method and Theory* vol. 6, edited by M. B. Schiffer, 1–51. New York: Academic Press.

———. 1985. "North American Archaeology and Archaeologists 1879–1934." *American Antiquity* 50: 249–260.

———. 1991. "On 'Paradigms' and 'Paradigm Bias' in Controversies over Human Antiquity in America." In *The First Americans: Search and Research*, edited by T. Dillehay and D. J. Meltzer, 13–49. Boca Raton, Fla.: CRC Press.

Meltzer, D. J., and R. C. Dunnell, eds. 1992. *The Archaeology of William Henry Holmes.* Washington, D.C.: Smithsonian Institution Press.

Morgan, L. H. 1877. *Ancient Society.* New York: Holt.

Nelson, N. C. 1906 [1996]. "Excavation of The Emeryville Shellmound, Being a Partial Report of Exploration for the Dep't. of Anthrop. during the Year 1906." In *Excavation of the Emeryville Shellmound, 1906: Nels C. Nelson's Final Report*, edited by J. M. Broughton, 1–47. University of California, Archaeological Research Facility, Contributions No. 54.

———. 1910. *The Ellis Landing Shellmound.* University of California, Publications in American Archaeology and Ethnology 7: 357–426.

———. 1913. "Ruins of Prehistoric New Mexico." *American Museum Journal* 13: 62–81.

———. 1916. "Chronology of the Tano Ruins, New Mexico." *American Anthropologist* 18: 159–180.

———. 1919a. "The Southwest Problem." *El Palacio* 6: 132–135.

———. 1919b. "Human Culture." *Natural History* 19: 131–140.

———. 1928a. "Review of 'The Antiquity of the Deposits of Jacob's Cavern' by V. C. Allison." *American Anthropologist* 30: 329–335.

———. 1928b. "In re Jacob's Cavern." *American Anthropologist* 30: 547–548.

———. 1932. "The Origin and Development of Material Culture." *Sigma Xi Quarterly* 20: 102–123.

———. 1937. "Prehistoric Archeology, Past, Present and Future." *Science* 85: 81–89.

O'Brien, M. J., and R. L. Lyman. 1998. *James A. Ford and the Growth of Americanist Archaeology.* Columbia: University of Missouri Press.

———. 1999. *Seriation, Stratigraphy, and Index Fossils: The Backbone of Archaeological Dating.* New York: Kluwer Academic/Plenum.

Peabody, C. 1904. "Exploration of Mounds, Coahoma County, Mississippi." *Peabody Museum of American Archaeology and Ethnology, Papers* 3 (2): 21–64.

———. 1908. *The Exploration of Bushey Cavern, near Cavetown, Maryland.* Phillips Academy, Department of Archaeology, Bulletin 4 (1).

———. 1910. "The Exploration of Mounds in North Carolina." *American Anthropologist* 12: 425–433.

Peabody, C., and W. K. Moorehead. 1904. *The Exploration of Jacobs Cavern, McDonald County, Missouri.* Phillips Academy, Department of Archaeology, Bulletin 1.

Pepper, G. H. 1916. "Yacatas of the Tierra Caliente, Michoacan, Mexico." In *Holmes Anniversary Volume: Anthropological Essays,* edited by F. W. Hodge, 415–420. Washington, D.C.: J. W. Bryan Press.

———. 1920. "Pueblo Bonito." *American Museum of Natural History, Anthropological Papers* 27.

Rowe, J. H. 1962. "Alfred Louis Kroeber, 1876–1960." *American Antiquity* 27: 395–415.

Schrabisch, M. 1909. "Indian Rock-Shelters in Northern New Jersey and Southern New York." In *The Indians of Greater New York and the Lower Hudson,* edited by C. Wissler. *American Museum of Natural History, Anthropological Papers* 3: 139–165.

Spier, L. 1913. "Results of an Archeological Survey of the State of New Jersey." *American Anthropologist* 15: 675–679.

———. 1916. "New Data on the Trenton Argillite Culture." *American Anthropologist* 18: 181–189.

———. 1931. "N. C. Nelson's Stratigraphic Technique in the Reconstruction of Prehistoric Sequences in Southwestern America." In *Methods in Social Science,* edited by S. A. Rice, 275–283. Chicago: University of Chicago Press.

Taylor, W. W. 1954. "Southwestern Archaeology, Its History and Theory." *American Anthropologist* 56: 561–575.

Uhle, F. M. 1907. "The Emeryville Shellmound." *University of California, Publications in American Archaeology and Ethnology* 7: 1–107.

Volk, E. 1911. "The Archaeology of the Delaware Valley." *Peabody Museum of American Archaeology and Ethnology, Papers 5.*

Will, G. F., and H. J. Spinden. 1906. "The Mandans: A Study of Their Culture, Archaeology and Language." *Peabody Museum of American Archaeology and Ethnology, Papers* 3 (4): 79–219.

Willey, G. R., and J. A. Sabloff. 1993. *A History of American Archaeology,* 3d ed. New York: Freeman.

Wilson, T. 1889. "The Paleolithic Period in the District of Columbia." *American Anthropologist* 2: 235–241.

———. 1895. "Paleolithic Man." *American Naturalist* 29: 599–600.

Wissler, C. 1915. "Explorations in the Southwest by the American Museum." *American Museum Journal* 15: 395–398.

———. 1916. "The Application of Statistical Methods to the Data on the Trenton Argillite Culture." *American Anthropologist* 18: 190–197.

Woodbury, R. B. 1960a. "Nels C. Nelson and Chronological Archaeology." *American Antiquity* 25: 400–401.

———. 1960b. "Nelson's Stratigraphy." *American Antiquity* 26: 98–99.

6

Leslie Spier and the Middle Atlantic Revolution That Never Happened

James Truncer

In 1914 and 1915, Alanson Skinner and Leslie Spier, employed at the American Museum of Natural History (AMNH) under Clark Wissler, carried out a brief renaissance of archaeological work at the by then well-known site of Abbott Farm near Trenton, New Jersey. Unlike earlier workers at the site (e.g., Abbott 1877, 1881, 1907, 1912; Holmes 1893a, 1893b; Volk 1911), Skinner and Spier did not attempt to assess the veracity of the American Paleolithic but focused instead on the so-called Argillite Culture, a label applied to the exclusively lithic assemblage of artifacts found in the "yellow sands." The yellow sands lay between the "black soil" above, thought to hold the remains of the Delaware Indians, and the famously controversial "Paleoliths" in the Trenton Gravels below. Despite continued interest in the artifacts and depositional history of the yellow sand (Abbott 1881, 1907, 1912; Holmes 1897; Volk 1894, 1911), it was still unclear in 1914 what, if any, affiliation the Argillite Culture had to the surrounding assemblages, although confidence in an American Paleolithic had waned significantly by the time Skinner and Spier commenced operations.

One year before he began excavations with Spier, Skinner (1913: 18) expressed the viewpoint of the AMNH: the remains in the yellow sand were pre-Delaware but not pre-Indian. To more fully examine the cultural content and depositional history of the yellow sand at Abbott Farm, Skinner and Spier opened three small trenches and a pit in May 1914. Working alone in October 1914, Skinner dug three additional large trenches, producing artifact distributions similar to those recorded earlier that spring. To test these distribution characteristics further, Spier returned to Abbott Farm in the summer of 1915, deepening and extending excavations in two of Skinner's trenches as well as recording the location of naturally occurring pebbles. Spier's work in the summer of 1915 was particularly innovative, attacking problems of site formation processes and chronology using sophisticated techniques for the time. As will become clear, however, Spier's attempt to develop a refined chronology occurred after the excavations were completed. The comprehensive results were published in 1918 as *The Trenton Argillite Culture*, an Anthropological Paper of the AMNH (Spier 1918a).

Spier's problem-oriented approach and analyses contrasts sharply with contemporary reconstructionist efforts in the region, such as Mark Harrington's (1924) investigation of *An Ancient Village Site of the Shinnecock Indians* on Long Island, published in same AMNH volume. Spier's work even looks different because his approach was statistical not ethnographic, a tack that allowed new kinds of questions to be addressed. Upon consulting with geologist Chester Reeds, Spier assiduously plotted the distribution and frequency of pebbles and artifacts both horizontally and vertically in order to quantitatively assess the mode and rate of artifact and sediment deposition. Establishing tight vertical control allowed Spier to eliminate the possibility that artifacts in the yellow sands had simply moved downward from the black soil, suggesting that they were not Delaware Indian material. In addition, Skinner and Spier's work confirmed previous observations that the yellow sand assemblage differed from the black soil assemblage. Notably absent were ceramic vessels, an observation recorded for deep strata at other sites in eastern North America (Harrington 1909; Nelson 1918).

Finally, Spier created projectile-point types from lithic materials recovered from the yellow sand and attempted to order them chronologically. This was the first American attempt to assign age to projectile-point forms based on vertical distribution. Previous researchers dismissed the notion of obtaining chronology from projectile-point form because this dimension was seen as arising from idiosyncratic processes or differences in raw materials and manufacturing ability (e.g., Fowke 1896; Rau 1876: 8–9; see Dunnell 1986: 159 for a discussion). Even stratigraphically documented lithic variability (e.g., Uhle 1907) was thought to represent only minor differences in manufacture (Kroeber 1909). Ceramic analysis fueled the breakthrough chronological work of Kidder (1916), Kroeber (1916), Nelson (1916), and Spier (1917) in the Southwest, and presumably Spier sought to emulate his and other's success in ordering southwestern ceramic styles by constructing types of projectile points found at

Abbott Farm. Deriving chronology from lithics however, proved to be inherently more difficult than in the case of ceramics because the former generally contain fewer stylistic attributes.

Despite an insistence on assigning variation to cultural stage constructions (e.g., Argillite Culture, Delaware Culture, etc.) and describing change as epochal or qualitative by noting the presence or absence of a trait such as pottery, Spier's attempt to chronologically order *kinds* of projectile points based on frequency change allowed for the possibility that minor cultural change and variation could be quantified. As noted by Lyman et al. (1997), this marks a distinct break in scale of analysis and in metaphysic from essentialism (change viewed as stages) to materialism (change viewed as continuous). As might be gathered from the remarks above, however, the work at Abbott Farm represents a mix of these two ontological perspectives, aspects of which are evident in excavation and analysis as well as interpretation.

The Trenton Argillite Culture: Abbott Farm Revisited

Even with its promising direction and a brief flurry of controversy published in *American Anthropologist* (Spier 1916; Linton 1917), Spier's work at Abbott Farm made little impact on eastern North American archaeology at the time, and even less on the Middle Atlantic. Not a single citation of the work was made in *American Historical Anthropology, Essays in Honor of Leslie Spier* (Riley and Taylor 1967). What went wrong? Here I examine several factors that have contributed to the publication's obscurity. First, Spier's attempt to chronologically order projectile-point types failed, and the reasons for this failure are explored. Of no less importance, however, was the withdraw of AMNH-sponsored research in the area. In 1916, Clark Wissler sent Leslie Spier and Ralph Linton, another Argillite Culture investigator who had conducted work for the University Museum with Ernest Hawkes (Hawkes and Linton 1916, 1917), to the Southwest. This departure essentially marked the end of sustained prehistoric research conducted in the Middle Atlantic by large, nonstate institutions, a trend started by the Bureau of American Ethnology (BAE) earlier in the century when William Holmes stopped conducting investigations in the District of Columbia and surrounding areas.

The impact on Middle Atlantic archaeology was profound: no research addressed the subject of the Argillite Culture for over two decades. Indeed, practically no professional archaeology occurred in New Jersey until the mid-1930s. When efforts did resume, a very different brand of archaeology emerged under Dorothy Cross—one uninfluenced by Spier or subsequent developments in chronology. In some respects, Middle Atlantic archaeology has never really recovered. It seldom participates in dialogue at the national, let alone international, level. The consequences of breaking continuity in research proved harmful in this case because in the subsequent void no work built upon Skinner and Spier's success or addressed the shortcomings.

Some students of Spier (Taylor 1963; I. Rouse 1996 pers. comm.) have implied that the reason no further investigation of the Argillite Culture occurred was that Spier had shown that it did not exist. This is something of a misunderstanding. Spier (1916: 564) felt that the term *Argillite Culture* was a misnomer because not all lithic artifacts from the yellow sands were manufactured from argillite. In assessing the cultural affiliation of the materials, however, Spier is quite clear: artifacts from the yellow sands at Abbott Farm, although secondarily deposited along with pebbles, represent one culture, distinct from that of the Delaware Indian. "All of the objects from the yellow soil constitute a homogenous unit; that is, we have found nothing that we may not refer to as a single culture," he noted (1918a: 210). Until the AMNH quit the area, there was no shortage of interest in the Argillite Culture; the desire to date the age of the yellow sand deposit, for instance, was expressed as late as 1916 (Wissler 1916: 238). Further work by the AMNH at Abbott Farm ceased, however, and its resources were directed elsewhere. There was good reason to do so. The Southwest was exploding with methodological developments in chronology.

Publication of *The Trenton Argillite Culture* is unusual in that three years passed between the end of fieldwork and its appearance in print. Spier's *Zuñi Ruins* report was clearly given priority for publication in the AMNH Anthropological Papers since it appeared in 1917, only one year after fieldwork was completed. A preliminary report by Spier (1916) on the Trenton Argillite Culture did appear in *American Anthropologist* in 1916, but one of the main additions of the 1918 publication was the attempt to chronologically order projectile-point and blade types. The time lag in publication is informative because by 1918, Spier (1917, 1918b) had made seminal contributions to Southwestern chronology at Zuñi and on the Little Colorado. At Abbott Farm, Spier tried to identify "stylistic pulsations" by constructing projectile-point and blade types from artifacts collected in the years just prior to his critical Southwest experience.

At first, Spier (1918a: 201) dismissed the possibility that assessing the frequency of "various types of arrowheads and blades" from the yellow sand would be chronologically informative. He felt that the frequency of types would yield normal curves simply because all deposited materials larger than grains of sand, including both artifacts and pebbles, were found to be normally distributed. Later in the publication, however, he appears to have changed his mind and explores the possibility of vertical differentiation of point and blade types (Spier 1918a: 210). Unfortunately, the analysis is beset by difficulties commonly encountered when working with previously collected data. Data collected to answer one problem do not always serve to answer another, and this must have been painfully evident to Spier in 1918. Although he carefully documented artifact and pebble provenience to within 2 inches to assess depositional contexts (1918a: 181), it is apparent that his *types* of projectile points and blades were constructed later. There are probably several reasons why this happened. While the importance of documenting the vertical provenience of stylistic types of pottery was beginning to be realized (Nelson 1916), developing similar types for projectile points had lagged behind. Constructing comparable stylistic types for projectile points was difficult due to greater constraints in material and form and because attributes that are free to vary over time are generally restricted to only one part of the artifact: the base. Moreover, while documenting the vertical positions of point styles would have informed on cultural change, it would not have addressed Spier's central question of how the yellow sand and its contents were deposited. To answer this, Spier knew he needed to only document where objects, both natural and cultural, occurred. In addition, by the time Nelson was beginning to realize some success in documenting cultural change by looking at frequency change in pottery styles, Spier was already convinced that all materials in the yellow sand were normally distributed, diminishing the likelihood that Nelson's technique would provide useful information at Abbott Farm. The important point here is that Spier's types, because they were constructed after excavations had ceased, were not able to be tested for historical significance during the course of excavation as Nels Nelson was able to do (see O'Brien, this volume).

While Spier's blade types are really preforms or blanks devoid of style, his eight projectile-point types are remarkably similar to some general types recognized today (figs. 6.1 and 6.2). Indeed, Spier (1918a: 204) constructed his types using the kinds of initial sorting techniques that would be more formally described by Alex Kreiger (1944) 26 years later. Some difficulty in identifying stylistic attributes is apparent, however, such

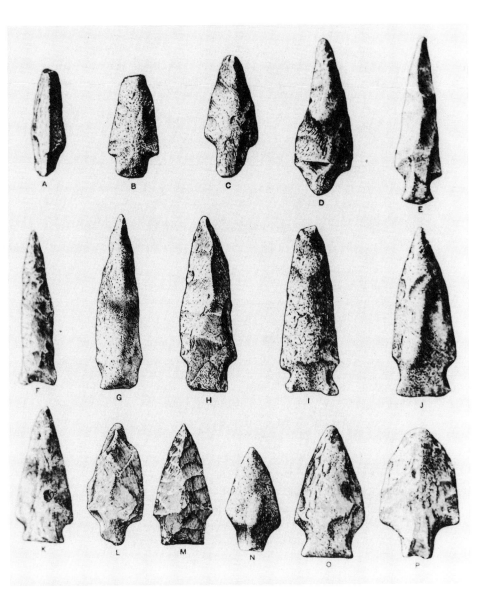

Fig. 6.1. Projectile point types as illustrated in Spier (1918a: 205). Type I: A–J (Poplar Island, Lackawaxen, Bare Island). Type II: K–P (Transitional Broadspear types).

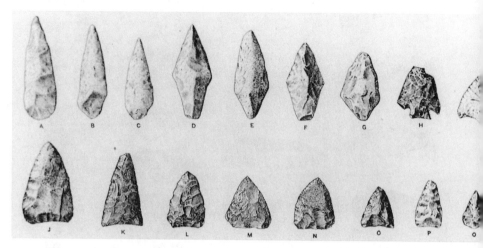

Fig. 6.2. Projectile point types as illustrated in Spier (1918a: 206). Type III: H and I (Brewerton Corner-Notched). Type IV: A–C (Lackawaxen Converging?). Type V: Q (Teardrop). Type VI: D–G (Rossville). Type VII: J–O (various triangular forms, some of which may be unfinished or broken: K and O resemble Madison and Levanna types, respectively). Type VIII: P (Madison).

as his tendency to rely on blade shape rather than basal attributes (Spier 1918a: 204, 208), and this mixing of homologous and analogous traits in constructing types surely hampered his results. Perhaps an even greater obstacle to Spier's analysis was the fact that Skinner's October 1914 excavations were profoundly different from those conducted in May of that year or those of Spier undertaken in the summer of 1915.

Spier is clear about the excavation procedures used at the different times. In May 1914, Skinner and Spier removed the uppermost black soil layer, after which "trenching proceeded by scraping the breast or forward face of the trench with a trowel" (Spier 1918a: 180) with horizontal and vertical measurements taken for each specimen encountered. Depth measurements were taken from "the plane of contact of black and yellow soils" (ibid.), which was now the surface. This was careful, meticulous excavation in which all artifacts were recovered by trowel and specimen numbers assigned to each recovered artifact (American Museum of Natural History, Division of Anthropology Archives [hereafter cited as AMNH/ANTH], Accession File 1914–32). The three trenches and single pit excavated in May amounted to the removal of about 1,800 cubic feet of sediment.

In October 1914, Skinner "commenced extensive excavations" (Spier 1918a: 180), opening three large trenches and sifting through almost 10,000 cubic feet of soil. This time he left the black soil intact and "excavated in levels, a foot at a time" (ibid.). The definition of a "level," however, rested on more than just a 1-foot measurement unit. As Spier relates, "The *uppermost level, 2 ft. deep in Trench A* and 1 ft. in Trenches B and C, including both black soil and yellow was arbitrarily segregated as being within a 'zone of doubt'" (ibid.; emphasis added). While Skinner's excavations may have proceeded "a foot at a time," artifacts were not assigned provenience in 1-foot arbitrary levels. Rather, Skinner lumped the artifacts into two stratigraphic units: the "zone of doubt" and the "yellow soil." Although these excavations produced "a large number of specimens" (ibid.), Spier does not mention any lateral or depth measurements being taken. Apparently the only depth information Skinner recorded was that of the two strata, an inference substantiated by Spier's reference to the distribution of artifacts recovered in October 1914 as a "gross distribution" (ibid.).

In 1915, Spier (AMNH/ANTH, Accession File 1915–53) had five immediate goals at Abbott Farm: (1) to determine whether the artifacts lay in more than one plane of deposition; (2) to determine if the artifacts lay in groups; (3) to determine if the artifacts in the yellow soil were always found distributed vertically in a characteristic manner; (4) to determine the position, extent and characteristics of the red bands; and (5) to define the relation of artifacts to certain geological features: (a) red bands, and (b) pebbles.

Note that chronology is largely incidental to the primary research goal of determining depositional processes. In extending Skinner's trenches, Spier (1918a: 180–181) reemphasized depth control: "The sand from the trenches was sifted a shovelful at a time and depths of specimens below the plane of contact were immediately recorded. The greatest error in these records due to the screening method is 2 inches." Thus, Spier was clearly using arbitrary levels to excavate in 1915, and it is likely that he was influenced by Nelson's (1916) use of arbitrary levels at San Cristóbal in the fall of 1914 since they were both employed at AMNH at the time (Lyman et al. 1997: 45). Spier (1918a: 181) also states that artifacts were recovered by troweling trench sections at Abbott Farm in 1915. Each artifact was assigned a specimen number, and depth in inches below the black soil was recorded (AMNH/ANTH, Accession File 1915–53). In all, Spier's work in 1915 returned to the May 1914 focus on obtaining fine-scaled depth information. Of course, there was a price to this meticulousness.

Even though Spier spent the summer (June–September) of 1915 digging, mapping, and recording at Abbott Farm, he ultimately examined only about 1,700–1,800 cubic feet of sediment, an amount similar to that processed during the May 1914 excavations.

Just why Skinner employed large stratigraphic units in October 1914 is not entirely clear (no report of these excavations is on file at AMNH/ANTH), but his odd-sounding term *zone of doubt* implies that his main concern was to qualitatively describe the contents of the underlying yellow soil (Skinner 1913: 18; Spier 1918a: 209) and minimize the possibility of contamination from ambiguous contexts. What Skinner "doubted" was the usefulness of any information obtained from outside the yellow sand, but the fact that soil color *graded* from black to yellow created a problem—was the layer in between black or yellow? Skinner's solution was conservative: one could only safely attribute artifacts to the Argillite Culture if they were definitely from the yellow sand, the rest could be lumped as non-Argillite Culture. Indeed, by combining the black soil and the "uppermost twelve inches or so" (Spier 1918a: 210) of yellow soil as the zone of doubt, it is clear that Skinner was not excavating according to natural stratigraphy based on color. Moreover, this lumping demonstrates that he was not interested in further distinguishing or documenting what was thought to be Delaware Indian material associated with the black soil. To Skinner, there was just the contents of the yellow soil and everything else; artifact-depth measurements were superfluous.

The methodological incongruities of the three excavation sessions at Abbott Farm in 1914 and 1915 had two major repercussions for Spier's projectile-point analysis. First, most of the projectile points that Spier had to work with (perhaps more than 80 percent) were recovered from excavations with the least amount of vertical depth control (Skinner's October excavations). Second, Skinner's conservative definition of yellow soil forced Spier to use Skinner's coarse vertical units ("zone of doubt" and "yellow soil") in plotting the absolute frequency of types (table 6.1). Even worse, when Spier combined his data with Skinner's, these vertical units no longer remained mutually exclusive. As Spier (1918a: 210) relates, the zone of doubt included the uppermost 12 inches of yellow soil (in addition to black soil), and the yellow soil artifacts came from a wider, unspecified vertical range from within the yellow sand, *including* the zone of doubt. Spier (1918a: 210) was cognizant of the problem of sample size and the less-than-optimal solution of merging the two data sets: "It would be interesting if there was *a sufficient number of specimens* to see whether there is any vertical differentiation of types. The tabulation of the [projectile-

Table 6.1. Absolute frequencies of projectile point types from the "zone of doubt" and "yellow soil"

Group	Arrow-heads							
	I	II	III	IV	V	VI	VII	VIII
From yellow soil	17	11	2	7	2	4	7	1
From "zone of doubt"	35	13	3	3	0	13	15	1
Totals	52	24	5	10	2	17	22	2

Reproduced from Spier 1918a: 204.

point and blade types based on Skinner's stratigraphic dichotomy] gives us *something of the sort*" (emphasis added). In combining Skinner's yellow soil artifacts with his, Spier (1918a: 204) was able to say that 66 artifacts were "definitely recorded from the yellow sand." When considering depth, however, he was obliged to accept that some of *his* upper yellow sand material actually fell within Skinner's zone of doubt level. These overlapping units obviously helped to further obscure differences in the vertical distribution of his types.

In comparing the absolute frequencies of point types between the two vertical units, Spier (1918a: 210) claimed that "there is no significant difference between the groups." However, the mixed analogous and ho-mologous attributes in his types and the overlapping vertical units he used would have helped to blur any such differences. Even so, some differences are noticeable (table 6.1), for instance more than twice the number of triangular points (Type VII) and more than three times the number of Type VI (Rossville-like) points occurred in the shallower zone of doubt level. In addition, more than twice the number of Type IV (Lackawaxen-like) points occurred in the deeper yellow soil. Why these differences did not appear significant to Spier is uncertain, although it is apparent that Skinner's coarse vertical categories forced Spier back into an essentialist conception of culture change, one concerned with difference rather than frequency change. The upshot was that while Spier determined how the yellow sand materials were deposited, he was unable to derive chronology from the previously collected lithic artifact assemblage. If Skinner had taken artifact-depth measurements in October, Spier might have been able to derive chronology from the types he constructed later using a kind of percentage stratigraphy (Lyman et al. 1998). Middle Atlantic archaeology would have changed overnight. Unfortunately, this did not happen. Spier and Linton were sent to the Southwest in 1916, soon to remove themselves from archaeological fieldwork altogether. Skinner left the AMNH in 1915 and never returned to Abbott Farm. Ernest Hawkes worked alone one last summer in southern New Jersey in 1916, but little new information was added. Modest state funding given to the Geological Survey of New Jersey for archaeological work dried up after 1915. Both C.C. Abbott and Ernest Volk died in 1919. New Jersey archaeology foundered for almost two decades.

The Archaeology of Dorothy Cross

In the mid-1930s and early 1940s, Dorothy Cross was funded by the WPA to excavate 40 sites throughout New Jersey over the course of almost five years. She would adopt what can be described as a hyper-short chronological perspective, a view that all non-European artifacts *were* the remains of historic tribes known to the area (Cross 1941). This radical stance went well beyond the short chronology position that can be attributed to William Henry Holmes (cf. Dent 1995: 42, 46). In fact, Holmes was perfectly willing to concede the existence of culturally (but not biologically) distinct prehistoric groups, suggesting in 1897 that initial inhabitation of eastern North America occurred somewhere between 500 and 5,000 years ago (Holmes 1897: 825). For Cross, all non-European artifacts found in New Jersey were attributable to the historically known Lenapé Indian tribe.

Since Cross's formal training and doctoral research focused on Middle Eastern archaeology (Ehrich 1973), it is difficult to know who may have influenced her approach to Middle Atlantic archaeology, although she mentioned that the Archaeological Society of New Jersey, composed largely of avocational archaeologists, acted in an advisory capacity (Cross 1941: iii–iv). It is also apparent from her 1941 publication (also see Richards 1939: 348n. 7) that she had extensive contact with geologists working at the New Jersey State Museum (her place of employment) and other New Jersey institutions. Some aspects of her analysis, however, such as averaging depths across sites, appears to be unique. What is clear is that she consistently rejected the notion of a pre-Delaware or pre-Lenapé culture put forward more than twenty years earlier.

Cross's short time-depth was based primarily on her assumption that artifacts found on the surface, regardless of site location and varying erosional and depositional histories, were very recent in age. The ground surface became a baseline against which intersite assemblages were compared; depth-below-surface measurements for material and artifact types were averaged and, in addition to their greatest recorded depth, used to assess their chronological relationships (Knowles 1941: 185–206) (Nathaniel Knowles was project supervisor for the Indian Site Survey from 1939 to 1940 and presented an analysis of artifact distribution in Cross's 1941 work). Since almost every material and artifact type was found on the surface at some point during the survey, time-depth was virtually eliminated. When material or artifact type frequencies differed stratigraphically within a site, or if such differences were observed between sites, these were explained as having resulted from postdepositional processes (e.g., human removal, wind action, and slope wash) acting differentially on material remains (Knowles 1941: 192–193). Although Cross was clearly aware of Spier's work at Abbott Farm, she failed to see any significant frequency change in her "chipped implement" types across depth of deposition, despite a total sample size of around 5,000 projectile points. Cross, unlike Spier, never attempted to plot the frequencies of her types by depth. Rather, the depths for each type were averaged, the greatest depth was noted, and then these data were compared (Knowles 1941: 195).

By 1941, the work of Dorothy Cross was seen as an anomaly in professional archaeology (see reviews: Bullen 1946; Carpenter 1942; Ritchie 1943), uninfluenced not only by Spier's (1918a) attempt to apply percentage stratigraphy at Abbott Farm but by the chronological work emerging in the East generally (e.g., Collins 1927; Ford 1936, 1938; Ritchie 1932a, 1932b, 1936, 1938; Willoughby 1935). Cross did recognize that Ritchie's (1938) Coastal Aspect closely resembled most of the materials recovered in her excavations, but because of the perceived "homogeneity of the New Jersey culture" she rejected the temporal implications of an Early and Late Focus (Cross 1941: 210–212), preferring instead to emphasize perceived minor cultural differences between northern and southern New Jersey. Cross noted that six traits recovered in the New Jersey survey were assigned by Ritchie to the Laurentian Aspect, but in relying on the ground surface as an age indicator, she asserts that "these traits when found in New Jersey appear to be well integrated in the culture as a whole and lack the chronological implications they appear to have elsewhere" (Cross 1941: 212).

To be fair, Cross was out of the loop. With the exception of Yale's Irving Rouse, she appears to have been offered very little in the way of professional mentoring. Just how much of this was due to her lack of background in American archaeology or personality is hard to say, but as practically the only woman archaeologist working in the area, the possibility of discrimination cannot be ruled out. She was not invited, for instance, to a conference on the "Woodland pattern" sponsored by the University of Chicago in 1941, although William Ritchie from the neighboring state of New York attended. In the end, many of the hard-won gains achieved two decades earlier by Spier and others were refuted on faulty grounds. New Jersey archaeology remained underdeveloped.

Conclusions

While Leslie Spier's *Trenton Argillite Culture* publication is infrequently cited, the work stands as an early and innovative attempt to assess artifact deposition. Due to the scientific nature of the research, his results can be empirically tested today. Breaking the continuity of Spier's line of inquiry created a void that was quickly filled by an undercurrent "common-sense" perspective—the view that all non-European artifacts were the remains of historic tribes, a position that probably dates back to times of European colonization. This layman's conception of chronology slipped into professional publication through the work of Dorothy Cross, who adopted a hyper-short chronological perspective because this was the position of the Archaeological Society of New Jersey, an institution she relied on heavily out of necessity for support and advice. One thing is clear: discontinuing AMNH research at Abbott Farm had a damaging effect on the trajectory of New Jersey archaeology. The withdrawl of BAE support had a similar effect on the archaeology of the Chesapeake Bay area, where a hyper-short chronology also came to the fore (Dent 1995: 42–49).

Had Spier been able to chronologically order his projectile-point types, all would have been different. He was not able to do so because new data were required, data that actually were collected in the spring of 1914 and the summer of 1915, but not by Skinner in October 1914. Unfortunately, Skinner's October excavations provided most of the data that Spier had to work with.

The events that unfolded at Abbott Farm during the teens have some serious implications for conducting archaeology today. Once dropped, a line of research inquiry cannot be expected, twenty years later, to resume from where it was left. Indeed, it took Skinner only four months to employ a radically different methodology at Abbott Farm, one that contrasted markedly with work conducted earlier that year at the same site, by the same institution, with identical research goals. Similar forms of research discontinuity plague archaeology today, a situation created not only by changing institutional agendas and inadequate funding but also by our general inability to build cumulative archaeological knowledge in an era of diverse and disconnected theoretical approaches. New direction in research is not necessarily undesirable in and of itself; the question is whether cumulative knowledge is being built. In order to build cumulative knowledge, archaeological research must produce empirically testable hypotheses using variables that are theoretically justified. Such an approach can engage national dialogue, even in a time of theoretical discord, by taking up issues that crosscut theoretical or regional interests. While concerted archaeological discussion of formation processes was still 60 years away, Spier's variables were geologically appropriate. His work at Abbott Farm briefly drew national attention because it addressed the age of human occupation in America and artifact depositional processes in new but empirically sound ways. In short, Spier's work can be assessed because he provided a means to be wrong. Later research in the area failed to adequately address, let alone build on, his work or attend to issues of wider interest, severely limiting the acquisition of new knowledge and, in the end, losing the national spotlight.

References

Abbott, C. C. 1877. "On the Discovery of Supposed Paleolithic Implements from the Glacial Drift in the Valley of the Delaware River, near Trenton, New Jersey." *Peabody Museum of American Archaeology and Ethnology, Annual Report of the Trustees* 2: 30–43.

———. 1881. *Primitive Industry.* Salem, Mass.: George A. Bates.

———. 1907. *Archaeologia Nova Caesarea.* Trenton, N.J.: MacCrellish and Quigley.

———. 1912. *Ten Years' Diggings in Lenápè Land, 1901–1911.* Trenton, N.J.: MacCrellish and Quigley.

Bullen, R. P. 1946. Review of *Archaeology of New Jersey,* vol. 1. *Bulletin of the Massachusetts Archaeological Society* 8: 8–10.

Carpenter, E. 1942. "The Archaeology of New Jersey by Dorothy Cross." *Pennsylvania Archaeologist* 12: 39–40.

Collins, H. B., Jr. 1927. "Potsherds from Choctaw Village Sites in Mississippi." *Journal of Washington Academy of Sciences* 17 (10): 259–261.

Cross, D. 1941. *Archaeology of New Jersey,* vol. 1. Trenton: Archaeological Society of New Jersey and the New Jersey State Museum.

Dent, R. J., Jr. 1995. *Chesapeake Prehistory: Old Traditions, New Directions.* New York: Plenum.

Dunnell, R. C. 1986. "Methodological Issues in Americanist Artifact Classification." *Advances in Archaeological Method and Theory,* vol. 9, edited by M. B. Schiffer, 149–207. New York: Academic Press.

Ehrich, R. W. 1973. "Dorothy Cross Jensen, 1906–1972." *American Antiquity* 38: 407–410.

Ford, J. A. 1936. "Analysis of Village Site Collections from Louisiana and Mississippi." *Department of Conservation, Louisiana State Geological Survey, Anthropological Study* 2. New Orleans.

———. 1938. "A Chronological Method Applicable to the Southeast." *American Antiquity* 3: 260–264.

Fowke, G. 1896. "Stone Art." In *Thirteenth Annual Report, Bureau of American Ethnology*, 57–178. Washington, D.C.: U.S. Government Printing Office.

Harrington, M. R. 1909. "The Rock Shelters of Armonk, New York." In *The Indians of Greater New York and the Lower Hudson*, edited by Clark Wissler. *American Museum of Natural History, Anthropological Papers* 3: 167–179.

———. 1924. "An Ancient Village Site of the Shinnecock Indians." *American Museum of Natural History, Anthropological Papers* 22 (5): 227–283.

Hawkes, E. W., and R. Linton. 1916. "A Pre-Lenape Site in New Jersey." *University of Pennsylvania Anthropological Publications* 6 (3): 47–77.

———. 1917. "A Pre-Lenape Culture in New Jersey." *American Anthropologist* 19: 487–494.

Holmes, W. H. 1893a. "Are There Traces of Man in the Trenton Gravels?" *Journal of Geology* 1: 15–37.

———. 1893b. "Gravel Man and the Paleolithic Culture: A Preliminary Word." *Science* 21: 135–136.

———. 1897. "Primitive Man in the Delaware Valley." *Science* 6: 824–829.

Kidder, A. V. 1916. "Archaeological Excavations at Pecos, New Mexico." *National Academy of Sciences, Proceedings* 2: 119–123.

Knowles, N. 1941. "Vertical Distribution of New Jersey Artifacts." In *Archaeology of New Jersey*, by D. Cross, vol. 1, 185–206. Trenton: Archaeological Society of New Jersey and the New Jersey State Museum.

Krieger, A. D. 1944. "The Typological Concept." *American Antiquity* 9: 271–288.

Kroeber, A. L. 1909. "The Archaeology of California." In *Putnam Anniversary Volume*, edited by Franz Boas, 1–42. New York: Stechert.

———. 1916. "Zuñi Potsherds." *American Museum of Natural History, Anthropological Papers* 18 (1): 1–37.

Linton, R. 1917. "Review of *A Pre-Lenape Site in New Jersey*: A Reply." *American Anthropologist* 19: 144–147.

Lyman, R. L., M. J. O'Brien, and R. C. Dunnell. 1997. *The Rise and Fall of Culture History*. New York: Plenum.

Lyman, R. L., S. Wolverton, and M. J. O'Brien. 1998. "Seriation, Superposition, and Interdigitation: A History of Americanist Graphic Depictions of Culture Change." *American Antiquity* 63: 239–261.

Nelson, N. C. 1916. "Chronology of the Tano Ruins, New Mexico." *American Anthropologist* 18: 159–180.

———. 1918. "Chronology in Florida." *American Museum of Natural History, Anthropological Papers* 22 (2): 74–103.

Rau, C. 1876. *From Being to Becoming: Time and Complexity in the Physical Sciences.* New York: Freeman.

Richards, H. G. 1939. "Reconsideration of the Dating of the Abbott Farm Site at Trenton, New Jersey." *American Journal of Science* 237: 345–354.

Riley, C. L., and W. W. Taylor. 1967. *American Historical Anthropology: Essays in Honor of Leslie Spier.* Carbondale: Southern Illinois University Press.

Ritchie, W. A. 1932a. "The Algonkin Sequence in New York." *American Anthropologist* 34: 406–414.

———. 1932b. "The Lamoka Lake Site." *Researches and Transactions of the New York State Archaeological Association* 7 (4). Rochester.

———. 1936. "New Evidence Relating to the Archaic Occupation of New York." *Researches and Transactions of the New York State Archaeological Association* 8 (1). Rochester.

———. 1938. "A Perspective of Northeastern Archaeology." *American Antiquity* 4: 94–112.

———. 1943. "Archaeology of New Jersey, Volume I, by Dorothy Cross." *American Anthropologist* 45: 130–132.

Skinner, A. 1913. "Types of Indian Remains Found in New Jersey." In *A Preliminary Report of the Archaeological Survey of New Jersey.* Geological Survey of New Jersey, Bulletin 9, 9–33. Trenton, N.J.: MacCrellish and Quigley.

Spier, L. 1916. "Review of 'A Pre-Lenape Site in New Jersey.'" *American Anthropologist* 18: 564–566.

———. 1917. "An Outline for a Chronology of Zuñi Ruins." *American Museum of Natural History, Anthropological Papers* 18 (3): 207–331.

———. 1918a. "The Trenton Argillite Culture." *American Museum of Natural History, Anthropological Papers* 22 (4): 167–226.

———. 1918b. "Notes on Some Little Colorado Ruins." *American Museum of Natural History, Anthropological Papers* 18 (4): 333–362.

Taylor, W. W. 1963. "Leslie Spier, 1893–1961." *American Antiquity* 28: 379–381.

Uhle, F. M. 1907. "The Emeryville Shell Mound." *University of California, Publications in American Archaeology and Ethnology* 7: 1–107.

Volk, E. 1894. "Observations on the Use of Argillite by Prehistoric People in the Delaware Valley." *Proceedings of the American Association for the Advancement of Science,* pp. 312–317.

———. 1911. "The Archaeology of the Delaware Valley." *Papers of the Peabody Museum* 5. Cambridge, Mass.

Willoughby, C. C. 1935. *Antiquities of the New England Indians.* Cambridge, Mass.: Peabody Museum.

Wissler, C. 1916. "The Present Status of the Antiquity of Man in North America." *Scientific Monthly* 2: 234–238.

7

George Langford at the Fisher Site, 1924–1929

Pioneer Stratigraphic Studies in the Midwest

Andrew L. Christenson

> The mounds are distinctly stratified, a most unusual occurrence.
> Their construction broadly resembles a chocolate cake, the earth
> layers being separated from each other by thin dark seams of
> mineralized vegetable matter with grass and weeds at the surface
> taking the place of frosting.
> —Langford 1928b: 247

Midwestern Archaeology in the Early Twentieth Century

Prior to 1924, the existence of sequential occupation levels in an archaeo-logical site in the midwestern United States had been poorly documented. Frederic Ward Putnam (1882, 1883) had noted stratigraphy at two mounds in Ohio, there were a couple of instances noted in Indiana (Black 1961; Homsher 1884), Duren Ward identified three "types" of burials by level at an Iowa mound (Ward 1905: 433), W. C. Mills (1902) noted two "periods" at the Adena Mound, and William B. Nickerson had noted stratigraphy in northwestern Illinois (Bennett 1945; Nickerson 1908: 87; 1912: 80). Even without stratigraphic observations, J. F. Snyder was able to suggest a cultural sequence in Illinois (Fowler 1962: 184). These find-ings, however, were not well known—shells cast up on the shore only to be washed away again, to use Schnapp's (1997: 36) analogy. Forgetting or ignoring Putnam's and Mills's findings, Henry Shetrone (1920: 161) noted the lack of stratification in Ohio sites and had to use various cultural characteristics to suggest a cultural sequence for the area. Two years later, after noting a few exceptions, Clark Wissler concluded that "we can truth-fully say that so far, archeological work outside of the regions of higher culture [i.e., Peru, Central America, the Southwest] has given negative stratification" (1922: 293).

It is difficult to understand what exactly midwestern archaeologists needed to get them moving in the study of culture history. Virtually *any* archaeologist who excavated a mound in the Midwest had "seen" stratigraphy, in the sense of soil color changes that were the result of temporal differences. While much of this stratification was the result of fairly short term activities in the construction of the mound (e.g., Nickerson 1908), some was the result of substantial time differences. If finding stratigraphy to document cultural difference or change was a significant research problem for midwestern archaeologists in the first quarter of the twentieth century, then they could have pursued that research almost anywhere. Clearly it was not.

Although it was recognized that there were different "cultures" in the region that were not contemporaneous, sites do not seem to have been selected for excavation because of their potential for having sequential occupation, as was done by Nelson and Kidder in the Southwest (Browman and Givens 1996: 87; Lyman and O'Brien 1999: 97). Sites were selected primarily because they had large features (i.e., mounds), because they had potential to yield burials (mounds), or in a few cases, because they were going to be destroyed (usually mounds). The discovery of stratification at the Fisher site in northern Illinois was the fortuitous conjunction of an observant and strong-willed man with a unique archaeological site that was threatened by farming. This chapter is an examination of that conjunction and its consequences.

Langford Excavates the Fisher Site

George Langford was trained in mechanical engineering at Yale University's Sheffield Scientific School and graduated in 1897. He had early experience in the West that gave him familiarity with American Indian life, had dug up Indian burials in Minnesota as a teenager (Langford 2001: 6), and had a passion for collecting fossils that remained with him all of his life. Langford first visited the Fisher site in 1898 and moved to Joliet shortly thereafter (Kullen 2000; Langford n.d.a: 2).[1] Located on the Des Plaines River just east of the junction of the Kankakee River, the site consisted of a series of burial mounds, large and small, with a surrounding village.[2]

It was not until November 1906 that Langford and a friend dug into one of the mounds and discovered a historic period skeleton. Amazingly,

Fig. 7.1. Langford (*right*) and Tennik at the Fisher site. By permission of the Laboratory of Anthropology, University of Illinois at Urbana–Champaign.

all of Langford's digging was done with one arm, as he had lost his left arm in a factory accident shortly after moving to Joliet. He did more digging at the site in 1912 and 1918. His 1912 notes indicate that they found skeletons in three tiers, or layers, and that the skeletons in those superimposed burials had different head shapes (Langford 1927: 156–157; 2001: 7), but he did not immediately pursue this phenomenon. About the same time his fossil collecting brought him into contact with the University of Chicago and other institutions (Langford 1964: 1–9) and gave him experience in excavating and reconstructing bones that would be useful later.[3] In the early 1920s, the Fisher site was threatened with destruction by plowing, and it was at this time that Langford began what would be five years of work at the site. Langford was thus one of the Midwest's pioneer salvage archaeologists (Kullen 2000).

Langford tried to get the American Museum of Natural History and the Field Museum interested in the site, and although they were supportive of his work, they were not interested in committing to any digging themselves (Langford 1961: 28–29). So Langford began on his own with the assistance of his Hungarian foreman, Albert Tennik (fig. 7.1), and sometimes his son or another mill worker. Of Albert, Langford said, "He won't take money from me although I have offered it several times. He likes my coffee, he likes the drive and he likes to dig when he finds something. He seems to understand that we are in the midst of discoveries that may produce valuable results scientifically" (Langford 1930c: 23, entry dated Nov. 4, 1924).

Except for having to "calm him down" occasionally to keep him from overly energetic digging (1930c: 14), Langford had found the perfect digging companion. They generally worked on Sundays and holidays at the site, which was a 17-mile drive (about 40 minutes) from his home, although they sometimes took off early from work during the week as well. By September 1924, when Langford and his associates began excavation, the Big East and Big West Mounds were about 1 foot lower and 10 percent larger than when visited in 1912. Langford planned to do some digging at the site to see what was there, then call it quits after a couple months' work. What happened next is best explained in his words, written years after the events described:

While excavating in the Big East Mound during the late Fall of 1924, Albert Tennik and I had no idea of continuing indefinitely. We planned to quit in November, as we had already found enough to get a fair picture of the mound and its contents. By this time I had become curious about certain "seams" or layers which persisted in our diggings but not enough so to continue into cold weather. So on Nov. 12 [Nov. 2 in Langford's field diary], 1924, we decided to make one more large excavation and end it.

But something occurred to change our minds. We found human burials with two copper celts and chipped flints, some of which were 3 1/2 feet above [the pre-mound] ground level. The "Black Seam," a charred earthy layer, previously noted, continued without interruption through the excavation. At a depth of 6 feet we encountered what appeared to be the clean underlying gravel but it seemed slightly discolored in one place. We dug there and found the crouching skeleton of a man, at a depth of 8 1/2 feet. Nothing was buried with him. We had to break through a hard and tough earth and ash layer to reach this burial. We thought we had reached the end of things but dug deeper anyhow in the clean undisturbed gravel and were astonished to find the crouching skeleton of a man, EM26, 4 ½ feet below [the pre-mound] ground level.

So we had a third tribe to consider, for this "concealed burial" was evidently something different from anything we had yet met with.

And we could see that the mound was stratified like a chocolate cake; made up of three thicker layers separated by two thinner layers or "seams." (Langford n.d.a: 15)

What Langford had found was a situation where an earlier group buried their dead in the glacial gravels (Lower Level). Later, burials were placed in an artificial mound built above the gravels (Middle Level), and this mound was in turn increased in height for the deposition of further burials (Upper Level). Langford believed the black seams were evidence of periods when the mound surfaces had vegetation on them (fig. 7.2). That Langford recognized the importance of the situation immediately is indicated by the excitement in his field diary, which begins, "A remarkable day" (Langford 1930c: 19).

All of the burials in the three levels that he identified were either not accompanied by grave goods or were accompanied by grave goods of non-European manufacture and were considered to be prehistoric. Langford did not make too much of the fact initially because he was primarily interested in prehistoric remains, but the mounds also had historic period burials that had attracted him to dig at the site in the first place. He came back to these remains in the late 1920s after the prehistoric mounds had pretty much been excavated (Langford 1930c). One of the mounds on the site had only historic period burials and was considered to be the first such mound documented ("Recent Mound-Builders" 1928; Langford n.d.a: 56). Langford did not spend much time on the question of which historic Indian group may have used the site, although he does say at one point that "New Yorkers would call this an Iroquoian culture although the non-Iroquoian pots would puzzle them" (Langford 1930c: 42–43). A study prepared for the Indian Claims Commission suggests that the burials in the East Mound were probably Potawatomi (Baerreis et al. 1974: 29).

Although he initially just used the ordinal terms for the three prehistoric levels, Langford later suggested the term *Fisher's* for the Middle

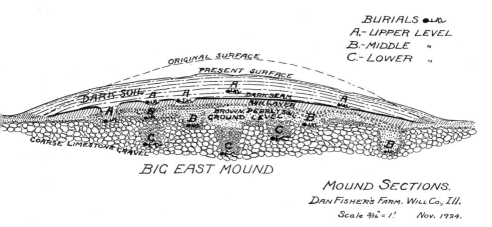

Fig. 7.2. Idealized cross-section of the Big East Mound at the Fisher site, drawn by Langford in 1924. From Langford (n.d.a.). By permission of the Illinois State Museum, Springfield.

Level and *Osborne's* for the level above it (Langford 1930b), the latter referring to the Kankakee River Refuse Heap, located on the Osborne property, which he had worked at a few years earlier (Langford 1919).

The large mounds were not the only features at the site to be stratified. In the habitation areas of the site what he called "food-holes," initially used for storage and later for refuse disposal, also showed stratification, as did the "pits," depressions representing the remains of structures. Langford's documentation of the site indicates that he recorded the microstratification of these features as well (Langford n.d.a: 75, 105; 1930d).

Excavation Techniques

Langford and Tennik were greatly hampered by the fact that the owner of the land the site was on, Dan Fisher, required that they backfill at the end of each day to keep livestock from getting injured (Langford 1961: 51). Langford mentions the Italian tenant coming down late one day to make sure that the holes were backfilled (Langford 1930c: 17, entry for Oct. 19, 1924), although they sometimes got away with leaving the pits open two or three days (Krogman 1927: entry for July 11). Perhaps in part as an adaptation to this requirement as well as being the quickest way to get below the surface, they usually dug holes, which looked like bomb craters, in the ground and placed the dirt around the perimeter where it could be easily shoveled back in (fig. 7.1). This technique had its hazards, as up to 12 feet of dirt could collapse, as happened on the day of the big discovery, with Langford barely avoiding burial (Langford 1930c: 22, entry for Nov. 2, 1924). On that day, Langford had chosen to dig a trench 17 feet long by 4 feet wide through one part of the East Mound, and thus had a larger cut than usual to discern soil differences (Langford 1930c: 19, entry for Nov. 2, 1924).

At times, excavation proceeded at a fast pace. In one day of excavation in the West Mound, eight burials were removed (Langford 1930c: 73–75, entry for October 31, 1926).

Based upon photographs, the primary excavation tools were fairly short-handled shovels with either broad straight blades (coal shovels) (fig. 7.1) or round pointed blades. A large pick is visible in one photograph and a small one in another. Although infrequently shown in photographs, awls, trowels, and brushes were used for finer work. Cigar boxes were used to pack small finds. A small round screen is shown in one photograph, but it is likely that screening was only done in special contexts. Langford had become interested in animal bones in his earlier work at the Kankakee River Refuse Heap, and the Fisher site is one of the few instances in early midwestern archaeology where faunal remains and bone tools were collected, analyzed, and saved for future examination (Parmalee 1962: 399).

Langford was a good indoor photographer but apparently had some difficulty with field photography because of "defective eyesight and inexperience with the camera" (Langford 1930c: 49), although his reports are illustrated by a number of photographs taken in the field. Langford had access to a transit for recording levels, and although he did not have a grid system, he had temporary control points from which he made his maps (Langford 1930c: 17).

The mounds were lettered and the pits were numbered. Each time they dug a new hole in a mound of pit, it was given a number (e.g., Hole No. 53) and plotted. Figure 7.3 shows Pit 19 with 10 holes and the date of excavation indicated for each. Burials (and associated specimens) were numbered sequentially for each mound. Langford developed a record system for burials and associated artifacts, 3EM19 being Burial 19 in the East Mound of Site 3 (Langford 1930c: 18), although eventually the site number was left off. The three main levels within the mounds were named ordinally—Upper, Middle, Lower—and zones within the levels were numbered with roman numerals or just designated "top" and "bottom." Langford took field notes and made maps and sketches as excavation pro-

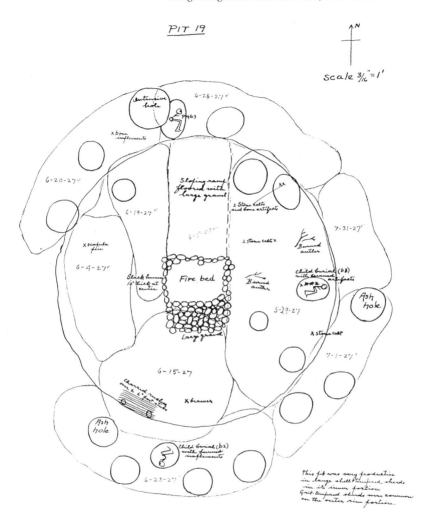

Fig. 7.3. Plan of Pit 19, showing features (*circles*) and excavation units (*elongated ovals*) with dates. This pit was excavated on ten separate days from May 29 to July 31, 1927. By permission of the Laboratory of Anthropology, University of Illinois at Urbana–Champaign.

ceeded (Langford 1961: 51). These were organized by provenience into notebooks and given to the University of Chicago with the collection (they are now at the Laboratory of Anthropology, University of Illinois at Urbana-Champaign).

Langford also put together several heavily illustrated "books" on the Fisher site long after he had retired from archaeology (Langford n.d.a, n.d.b). These are written in neat longhand, with numerous photographs and illustrations (figs. 7.2 and 7.3). He also produced typewritten notes on his 1928 and 1929 work at the site (Langford 1930a, 1930b), and near the end of his life he hand wrote a manuscript on Chicago area archaeology that featured the Fisher site (Langford 1961).

In addition to the problems of having only a short period of time to excavate, record, and refill each excavation, Langford had the typical problems of dealing with landowners and tenants. After the Fishers had moved to Joliet and left the farming to a tenant, Langford tried to buy the site but was not successful (Langford 1961: 171). He was able to stop the plowing of the site and kept other diggers off, but in 1928, the farm was sold to a construction company to use for fill to construct a nearby dam. By intimidation and bluff, Langford was able to continue salvage work at the site for a year or so, but he was finally ordered off the property by company officials in July 1929 (Langford 1930b: 6; 1961: 171–172).

Analysis

Langford had a laboratory at his office at the steel plant, where he spent innumerable hours piecing together pottery, skulls, and other broken finds that are well illustrated in his reports (Langford 1927: plates 11–14, 21, 24–30). Anyone who has done such reconstruction work will appreciate what Langford had to contend with having only one arm.

Langford spent much time reconstructing pottery vessels and examining their designs (Langford 1927: plates 11–14). He also described and photographed the variety of shell, bone, stone, and metal (i.e., copper) artifacts that occurred with the prehistoric burials. He developed a projectile-point classification system, indicating careful thinking about the relationship of formal and functional variation (Langford 1937b) that received some professional notice (Greenman 1929: 83). What makes Langford's analysis of the Fisher site remains so different from most of his contemporaries was his careful reconstruction and measurement of human skulls and attention to details such as disease and trauma evidenced in the bones. His particular interest in the human skeletal remains may have come from his previous work reconstructing fossils, and it gave him a way to make archaeological interpretations even when there were no artifacts. His division of the Lower Level into two zones, and skeletal populations, is based solely upon soil differences and head-shape differences in the burials.

Although Langford was widely read in scientific literature, it is difficult to determine what specifically he read because he only occasionally refers to other people's work in his journal. The only publication mentioned in any of his articles is Hrdlička's *Anthropometry* (1920), which Langford used to make what appear to be the first set of such bone measurements made on an Illinois burial population (Langford 1927: table between 204 and 205). He also did facial reconstructions by building up clay on skulls and then making a plaster cast (Langford 1961: 48).

Site Dating and Interpretations

In the Upper Level (above the Black Seam) of the two big mounds at Fisher, Langford found short-headed skulls, notched or stemmed arrowpoints, and grit-tempered pottery (n.d.a: 26, 28; 1927: 188–189). The Middle Level of the mounds contained the bulk of the burials, which had primarily broad heads associated with small, triangular arrowpoints, copper and stone celts, and mostly shell-tempered pottery (Langford n.d.a. 26; 1927: 176, 201–202). The Lower Level remains kept Langford digging because, although they had few artifacts, the level appeared to have an earlier, long-headed population and a later meso-headed one (ibid.: 26, 31; 1927: 171).

Although in an early journal entry, Langford theorized that he might see one of the deep burials accompanied by some extinct animal (Langford 1930c: 43, entry for May 16, 1926), he speculated little on the age of the strata other than the obvious post-European contact dating of the shallowest burials with items of European manufacture. Although newspaper quotations need to be taken with a grain of salt, an article published after the excavation of Fisher was completed quotes Langford as claiming to have found seven races at the site, the oldest dating to 1000 B.C. ("St. Paul Boy's Hobby" 1930). Langford was certainly not a proponent of glacial man, although after the Peking Man finds were publicized in 1930, the National Research Council issued a bulletin to promote interest in the topic in the United States. The frontispiece showed Langford crouching over a Fisher burial that was only about 500 years old (Bentley 1931; Langford 1961: 105).

Langford clearly felt that the site showed a "succession of human occupation" indicating "cultural changes" (1927: 187), but he elaborated on the details very little. In general, he seems to have believed that each of these levels represents at least three "peoples" or three "cultures" that were "distinct racially and in their civilizations," and that the levels were separated by "long pauses in the construction" ("Earthworks" 1928; Langford 1927: 247; 1929: 80). When one counts the post-European contact burials at the top of the mounds and the two distinct head-shapes in the Lower Level, there would be five "cultures" or "peoples" represented.

Although not appearing in print, his "books" suggest that population replacement was not the only way he looked at the mound sequence, as he talks about "gradual change from shell-tempered to grit-tempered with the two types co-existing" and "gradual decline in elaborate decoration" (Langford n.d.a: 28). In the same book, he gives a chronology of Fisher, with A.D. 1800–1828 being the very latest evidence of Indian occupation and 800–900 being the lowest "concealed" burials with no artifacts (ibid.: 3), dates no doubt derived from later archaeological work (see Griffin 1946: 11; Wray 1952; and Markman 1991:78–87 for interpretations of the Fisher levels in the midwestern archaeological sequence).

Langford Presents Fisher to the Professional Archaeological Community

In 1924, Illinois and surrounding states had few active archaeological programs focused on local archaeology (Griffin 1976: 5–6; Jones 1976: xlv). Fay-Cooper Cole had just arrived at Chicago but had not started his archaeological training program. The Field Museum was not interested in local archaeology, and the University of Illinois did not yet have an archaeologist (A. R. Kelly arrived in 1929).[4] Thus, when an amateur archaeologist wanted advice and help with archaeological problems, he had to contact scholars outside the region.

Langford's communication with the American archaeological community about the Fisher site prior to late 1924 are not well documented, although Fisher site artifacts and burials were included in the "3 barrels and 2 boxes" of artifacts from the Joliet area that he donated to the American Museum of Natural History in 1919 (Langford 1964: 9). He had contacts with other major American museums because of his work making plaster bas-reliefs of European Paleolithic scenes and American megafauna. In 1919, one set went to the Peabody Museum of Natural History at Yale University, his alma mater, and two went to the American Museum of Natural History.[5] Later a set went to the University of Illinois.[6]

Langford's knowledge of the stratigraphic revolution that was taking place in American archaeology is also unknown. Interestingly, the first communication about the discoveries at the Fisher site that we have are a letter from Nels C. Nelson of the American Museum of Natural History dated February 2, 1925.[7] Nelson, of course, was known for his pioneering stratigraphic archaeology in New Mexico (Browman and Givens 1996) and has been called the first prehistorian to use stratigraphy to detect culture change (O'Brien 1996: 157). Nelson apologized for not answering sooner (indicating that Langford sent him materials perhaps in late 1924) but had to take a brief look at the photos while Mrs. Nelson read the description. This would indicate that Langford sent a fairly detailed description of the site with extensive photo documentation. Nelson's principal comment on the site is that the "chronological indications, European contact, long heads, round heads, etc., are all extremely suggestive but doubtless need more and wider investigation to establish them." Langford had apparently asked for assistance from the museum in excavating the site, and Nelson apologized that he was the only person at the museum with any interest in American archaeology but had to attend to the archaeology of the entire world without assistance. He indicated that the number of museums that might help were limited. "The Field Museum is interested everywhere else but in Illinois," he stated.[8] He suggested William C. Mills at the Ohio State Historical Society and the Museum of the American Indian, which he particularly recommended.[9] Langford apparently wrote both institutions, but this contact did not lead to any assistance.

Another contact was the founder of the American School of Prehistoric Research at Yale University, George Grant MacCurdy, a specialist in Paleolithic archaeology and human evolution. The Yale association was probably one reason for the contact, but MacCurdy had also recently published a book on human origins (MacCurdy 1924) and so would have been a logical contact concerning the Fisher skeletal material. Langford sent MacCurdy three photographs of Fisher bones that were acknowledged without specific comment.[10] Later that year, MacCurdy invited Langford to give a paper at the American Anthropological Association meeting at New Haven.[11] A year later, Langford arranged for MacCurdy to give a public lecture at the Joliet High School and to stay with the Langfords while he was there. This apparently occurred in January 1927, and MacCurdy was able to see Langford's collections and the Fisher site at that time, although there is no further correspondence between them in Langford's files.

One of Langford's most important contacts was Roland B. Dixon of Harvard University, who had recently completed a study of the races of humans that included much material on cranial shape (Dixon 1923). He was also founding chairman and longtime member of the Committee on State Archaeological Surveys of the Division of Anthropology and Psychology, National Research Council (Guthe 1930: 52–54; O'Brien and Lyman

2001). By early 1926, Langford had prepared a manuscript on his work at the Fisher site. At some point he sent a copy to Dixon, who recommended it highly to Robert Lowie for publication in *American Anthropologist*.[12] Dixon had one important comment on the paper: Langford had submitted an "ideal section" of the two large Fisher mounds that "does not exactly jibe with the written descriptions."[13] Dixon suggested that Langford include actual sections across the mounds, and these were included in the published article (Langford 1927: fig. 5). The published drawings of six sections of the two larger Fisher mounds are closer to what Langford actually saw in his side walls, although they are harder for the reader to figure out than an idealized section of the complete mounds would have been (compare fig. 7.2 and fig. 7.4). When Dixon visited the site in 1927, he "put a bug" in Langford's ear that the Fisher pits were Mandan. After looking at a paper on the Mandans by Will and Spinden, Langford decided that the pit dwellings were not similar, and neither was the material culture (Langford 1930d: 29).

Clark Wissler at the American Museum was another player in the Fisher site story. Langford had previously been in touch with him about his work at the Kankakee River Refuse Heap,[14] a site about which he had published an article a few years earlier (Langford 1919). Wissler had also been chairman of the Committee on State Archaeological Surveys (Guthe 1930: 53). He was a strong proponent of the "new archaeology," as he called stratigraphic excavation and seriation (Browman and Givens 1996: 85; Rowe 1975; Wissler 1917) and was also critical in promoting the search for chronology in the American Southwest (Nash 1999: 23; Snead 2001: 104–123). Wissler was enthusiastic about Langford's progress and noted, "You are, of course, aware that the establishment of such chronological distinctions is the most important thing in archaeology at present. It is only by the establishment of such horizons that archaeology can expect to take its place with geology and the other earth sciences."[15] Langford donated some Fisher site material to the American Museum later that year.[16]

After seeing a copy of Langford's Fisher report from another source, Alfred V. Kidder, who succeeded Wissler as chairman of the Committee on State Archaeological Surveys in 1924 (Guthe 1930: 53), wrote Langford and congratulated him on his work and stressed to him the importance of keeping his collection together.[17] Although hardly the first to observe strata or dig stratigraphically, Kidder is still credited with bringing stratigraphic excavation to the attention of American archaeology (Browman and Givens 1996; Guthe 1952: 2–3). The following year, Kidder invited

Fig. 7.4. Mound sections from East Mound, Fisher Site, as published in *American Anthropologist* (Langford 1927: fig. 5, *upper half*).

Langford to sit in on a meeting in Chicago of people interested in midwestern archaeology and arranged to visit the Fisher site (which occurred on March 20).[18] After the trip, he thanked Langford for the visit and said that he had requested the Peabody Museum to send Langford a copy of Willoughby's report on Madisonville and asked Langford to compare his material.[19]

Langford's largest extant correspondence is with Fay-Cooper Cole. Cole originally aspired to be an archaeologist but was forced by circumstances to drop the idea in favor of physical anthropology and ethnology (Stocking 1979: 2). He moved to the University of Chicago from the Field Museum in 1923 and soon began an archaeological survey of the state (Brose 1973: 97; Browman 2002; Haag 1986: 65). He saw archaeology as one means to gain support for a separate anthropology department at the university (Eggan 1974: 7) but also as an integral part of anthropological training (Jones 1976: xli).[20]

In the fall of 1926, Cole was looking for field opportunities for his students and apparently had Langford scouting for possible mound sites to excavate.[21] The next spring, Cole asked Langford to allow his students to come to Langford's house to see his collection and then go to the site.[22] Langford put the group of student to work on Pit 19. Of the students that came, Langford had Wilton Krogman and Wendell Bennett to most of the digging with he and Tennik, but one photo shows about ten people in the pit (Langford n.d.a: 77). They used the pitting excavation technique at that point, with backdirt piled closely so it could be put back in easily, but later on they "laid out two lines of stakes in 6 squares of 5' each" (Krogman 1927: entry for June 20). Langford and Tennik continued work on the structure after the Chicago group left, and Langford sent a copy of his notes to Cole a couple of days later.[23] All told, the Chicago group spent several weeks at the site that year, excavating two complete and four partial pits (Langford 1928a: 7).

That summer Cole wrote Langford about the possibility that Kidder would work with the Chicago group for a while in the field. He asked if they could come to Fisher to work and made it clear that they did not want to "but [sic] in."[24] Kidder spent a day with Cole and his students at Fisher (Kidder 1927). In September, Cole invited Langford to a conference at the University of Chicago to discuss the season's work and indicated that he would try to get Kidder to come as well, although there is no evidence that he did.[25]

The next year, Cole offered to present the results of Langford's work at the meeting of the Central Section of the American Anthropological Association in Beloit and invited Langford to attend. He also asked for permission for two of his students to come down to Joliet to "go over" Langford's collection and to make skeletal measurements.[26] Later in the year Krogman, Bennett, and another student came down and explored one of the pits, using the pitting technique again (fig. 7.5). Leslie Spier and some of his students worked at the site that summer as well.

In June and July 1928, at the suggestion of Langford, a party from the University came down to excavate a mound (Oakwood) within the cemetery at Joliet. Headed by Wilton M. Krogman, the group included Thorne Deuel, Fred Eggan, and Georg Neumann. Interestingly, when the Chicago students dug with Langford, they often used his pitting technique, but when they worked at Oakwood, they staked off the site in 5-foot squares and excavated a trench through the length of the mound. This latter method, derived from the work of W. B. Nickerson, who got it from F. W. Putnam, began to be used by Chicago in 1926 (Browman 2002: 261). This shifting of techniques may have been a case of "when in Rome," but it may

Fig. 7.5. Labeled "University of Chicago students exploring food holes in one of the Pits, 1928—W. Krogman, *left;* Ingram, *center;* W. Bennett, *right*" (Langford 1961: 128). This is probably in July 1927, and Langford's diary lists the students as Krogman, Bennett, and Engberg. George Langford Papers, by courtesy of Minnesota Historical Society, St. Paul.

in part have been a result of the luxury at Oakwood of not having to refill the excavations at the end of the day. Whether and how much Cole, Krogman, and the other Chicago archaeologists attempted to get Langford to use a more controlled excavation method is unknown, but he appears to have resisted.

Langford donated much of his Fisher site materials to the University of Chicago in 1930 and at the same time was made a Research Associate of the Department of Anthropology.[27] This year-long appointment was renewed for a long time after Langford had ceased to participate in archaeology.

Of course, Langford's widest communication with professional archae-ologists came from his publications. It is unclear the process that led to his first publication in the *American Anthropologist* (Langford 1919), but his contacts at the American Museum of Natural History and Clark Wissler are likely possibilities. By the time he had a manuscript ready on the Fisher site, he was known to the archaeological community and had contacts with prominent scholars who could provide useful feedback on the con-tents as well as recommend publication. Closer to home, he published two summaries of his work in the *Transactions of the Illinois State Academy of Science* (Langford 1928b, 1929). He was also a contributor (1927–59) to *Teocentli,* a newsletter created by a group of primarily professional ar-chaeologists, established by Carl Guthe, who sent biyearly (now yearly) summaries of their work to other members (McGimsey 1998).

Langford also received nationwide publicity in the news section of *Science* ("Indian Mounds of Illinois" 1926) and through a lead article (Thone 1926) and a shorter notice in *Science News-Letter* ("Earthworks" 1928), and in an article on amateur scientists distributed by Science Service ("Amateurs in Field of Science" 1926). These notices were particu-larly important because they were picked up by newspapers and maga-zines across the country. When J. W. Fewkes of the Smithsonian Institu-tion read the *Science News-Letter* article, he telephoned Kidder "in a state of considerable excitement," another indicator of what even at this late date the discovery of stratigraphy could do.[28]

Langford was apparently not a public speaker. One of the rare times Mrs. Langford is mentioned in his journal is when she read his paper at the meeting of the Illinois State Academy of Science in April 1927 (Langford 1930d; see also "Langford" 1927; paper published as Langford 1928b). In February 1929, he wrote Cole about the possibility of someone reading his paper at a meeting in Macomb in May,[29] and at a meeting of the Illinois State Historical Society in Joliet in October of the same year, someone else read his paper ("State History Society" 1929). He was not antisocial, however, as he gave tours of the site (75 people from the Academy of Science meeting of 1927 came to the site), talked to newspaper reporters, and accommodated many groups of University of Chicago students.

Langford's Stratigraphy

Nearly a decade after publication of Langford's work at the Fisher site, Fay-Cooper Cole and Thorne Deuel presented the results of the use of the "Chicago method" of excavation in their pioneering study of Illinois River

Valley archaeology. In it they made the following comment: "The old-time method of 'pitting' a mound by digging from the top is no longer employed by serious students of archaeology. The obliteration of all evidences of stratification, intrusions, and the like condemns this procedure" (Cole and Deuel 1937: 32n. 11). While this statement is generally true, Langford's "method," which this comment could be referring to, allowed him to record the strata at Fisher, often in considerable detail, that later excavations using the Chicago technique basically confirmed (Griffin 1946). Once he had seen the strata in the mounds, he spent considerable effort recording soil irregularities. "There is no question in my mind that the three seams enumerated [upper Black Seam, Ash Layer, lower Black Seam] are the main factors in this mound for determining its meaning stratigraphically and for finding the true relationship of one burial to another," he wrote. "My main task was to locate them correctly and not be misled by streaks and other local soil irregularities, a task requiring careful observation" (Langford 1927: 162).

Although he broke some rules of what would shortly be considered good archaeological method, Langford clearly understood the importance examining the relationships of cultural and natural features visible in the soil and did what appears to be a reasonably good job of it. His writings and drawings indicate that he had independently developed a version of the "two essential ideas to the theory of archaeological stratigraphy, namely: the value of the interface and the numbering of layers" (Harris 1982: 11), the backbone of the Wheeler-Kenyon system developed in detail in the 1930s. He also used the stratification to create a cultural/biological sequence for the site. Except for work at the Kankakee River Refuse Heap, which seemed to be a single component site, Langford had no theories about the culture(s) of the area that he was digging in, but was simply using the strata at the Fisher site to create a sequence.

Because of his paleontological interests, Langford was experienced at looking at strata and boundaries in the field. In a children's book published before his work at Fisher began, he explained to the reader the importance of rock "accumulations" in reconstructing the sequence of mammals in North America (Langford 1923: xiv) and used an ideal section of the earth as his table of contents with, in typical Langford creativity, page numbers in reverse order.

Two basic stratigraphic excavation techniques have been defined: the "bread loaf" technique and the "onion skin" technique (Lyman and O'Brien 1999: 63–64). Langford did not have the luxury of either of these methods; instead, he used a pitting technique. Initially, Langford and

Tennik simply dug down until they hit a burial. After doing this repeatedly, Langford noticed strata, seams that occurred repeatedly in the same
order within the mound. Once the importance of the seams, as boundaries
of thicker strata, became apparent, the issue of placing burials above or
below seams became primary, and Langford apparently spent much time
in making post facto stratigraphic interpretations (Browman and Givens
1996: 81). His method of digging allowed stratigraphic observations in
the side walls of his holes, and he could examine the relationship of the
burial pits to the general strata of the mounds (Langford 1927: 168).

Langford's (n.d.a: 108) claim that a "child could have read" the Fisher
site strata is belied by comments elsewhere on the difficulty of examining
and understanding the stratigraphic record. He did stratigraphic excavation, however, by removing burials and their accompanying artifacts in
associated lots and by keeping artifacts not associated with burials together by level. Thus it appears that Langford and Tennik's excavation
technique evolved from a simple potholing that was standard among relic
collectors (and some archaeologists) at the time to a crude, but fairly effective, mix of stratigraphic excavation by holes or trenches and post facto
observation.

Why did it take until the mid-1920s for an archaeologist to use stratification in a midwestern archaeological site to construct an archaeological
sequence? The long history of stratigraphic observations in the eastern
United States has already been noted. Even with scholars such as Holmes
and Hrdlička batting down claims of paleolithic sites in North America,
there was plenty of evidence of time-depth to allow for examination of the
record for a cultural sequence.

Taking Moorehead's nearly contemporaneous (1922–24, 1927) excavations at Cahokia as an example, we see stratigraphy commonly noted in
almost all of the mound cross-sections (Leighton 1923: 77–87; Moorehead 1929b: 35, 40, 51, fig. 9). Although some of these examples of stratification represent fairly short-term differences in mound fill during construction, others are evidence of sequences of much longer duration. In no
case does Moorehead use the stratification sequence to suggest a cultural
sequence, even when there were data to do so (Kelly 2000: 33–34).

Langford's discovery of a cultural sequence at the Fisher site, primarily
through the superposition of burials with associated grave goods, may be
an example of a postmature discovery (Zuckerman and Lederberg 1986).
To qualify as postmature a discovery "must have been technically achiev-
able prior to the time at which it was actually achieved, it must have been
comprehensible to working scientists at the [prior] time, and scientists at

the [prior] time must have been able to appreciate the implications of the discovery" (Hull 2002: 337–338). Although a case can be made for uniqueness or at least rarity of the Fisher site cultural sequence in the Chicago area (Doershuk 1988: 16; Markman 1991: 77, 78), there were certainly many other sites in Illinois and the Midwest that had such stratigraphy. For whatever reason, it took until the end of the first quarter of the twentieth century for an amateur archaeologist to encounter stratigraphy, observe stratigraphic differences in cultural and biological remains, and make enough noise to get professionals to come and see what he had found.

Langford's Influence

From shortly after his discovery of stratification at the Fisher site in late 1924 until at least the late 1920s, Langford's archaeological discoveries at the site were known to all of the significant players in eastern archaeology.[30] Copies of Langford's reports and photographs were in their files, articles by or about him were in major journals and regional newspapers, there were presentations at national meetings about his findings, and he was referenced by leading archaeologists (Cole 1932: 76; 1935: 42; 1936; Cole and Deuel 1931: 336; Moorehead 1929a: 550; 1930a: 50; 1930b: 26, 29; Shetrone 1930 [1941]: 317, 327–329). That being said, it is more difficult to find evidence of the influence of his findings upon archaeological practice or interpretation in the Midwest.

Guthe (1952: 2) argues for the importance of Kidder's *Introduction to the Study of Southwestern Archaeology* in making American archaeologists aware of stratigraphic excavation.[31] Although Lyman and O'Brien (1999: 61–62) make a case that stratigraphic awareness and even excavation was present in American archaeology from before the turn of the century, it appears that the use of clearly demarcated strata to make interpretations of cultural change at a single site was something most eastern archaeologists had little personal familiarity with. For archaeologists working in the midcontinent, Kidder's work may have been interesting but probably seemed somewhat distant, "beyond the pale" to use Neitzel's (1994: 137) phrase. The more immediate and culturally relevant work of Langford would have been more telling.

Although he was unable to show visitors a very long cross section of one of the Fisher mounds, Langford's notes, photographs, and competent demeanor had their effect. Visits to the Fisher site by MacCurdy, Dixon, Kidder, Guthe, Spier, and Cole are documented, and no doubt there were others. Cole's visits to and involvement with the Fisher site had a broad impact.[32] Many of the leading archaeologists of the 1930s and later were trained in his program (Browman 2002) and either visited or knew about the Fisher site. Two of Cole's early archaeology students discussed Langford's work in the light of the university's projects in the region (Eggan 1933; Krogman 1931). It is significant that these first discussions by professional (student) archaeologists of cultural/chronological sequences in Illinois were by people who worked with Langford at Fisher or Adler and who had as their only data for such sequences the Fisher site and the Adler mounds. By 1930, University of Chicago archaeologists were deep into the cultural sequence of Fulton County in central Illinois that lead to the classic volume *Rediscovering Illinois* (Cole and Deuel 1937). While it would certainly be an exaggeration to say that Illinois archaeology would not have been rediscovered if it had not been for George Langford, his unacknowledged legacy is the exposure of Cole and his students to excavation of well-defined but complex stratigraphy, an exposure that certainly made them better able to record and interpret such situations in other contexts.

Langford's excavations may also have contributed more broadly to the education of those who were digging sites. In the *Guide Leaflet for Amateur Archaeologists* issued by the Committee on State Archaeological Surveys in 1930 and written by Fay-Cooper Cole, Carl Guthe, A. V. Kidder, and Neil Judd (Cole and Deuel 1937: 24n. 3), there is the following statement: "It not infrequently happened that a mound was originally built by a people practicing one method of burial, but was later used by incoming tribes. Such intrusive burials are most instructive in deciphering the sequence of cultures" (National Research Council 1930: 5). It seems likely that this statement is to a large extent a result of Langford's Fisher site work, considering that three of the authors of the leaflet worked with him at the site and that Fisher was the best-known example of such a burial sequence.

Langford was a key player in the Illinois archaeological community, as indicated by his correspondence with professionals such as Cole and Moorehead and amateurs who wanted his advice or wished to obtain artifacts for their collections (it is unclear if Langford traded with other collectors). In a major "inspection" tour of the Mississippi Valley, Carl Guthe, chairman of the Committee on State Archaeological Surveys, attempted to inventory individuals or groups in eight states that had an interest in local archaeology. His comments on Illinois in a confidential report are revealing: "There are five centers of archaeological activity, two of which are prosecuted by private interest (Dickson and Langford). The

University of Chicago has two field parties, one on excavation, and one on survey work. The University of Illinois is conducting a survey of the Illinois River region. The methods are satisfactory, and the cooperative spirit among the various workers is strong. While the political situation offers no help, the work in the state is growing nevertheless" (Guthe 1928: 2).

That Langford and his volunteer associates qualified as a "center of archaeological activity" indicates the remarkable amount of work he accomplished in a small area—but also the fairly primitive state of Illinois archaeology at the time.

Warren Moorehead, on loan from the Phillips Academy to the University of Illinois to conduct archaeological work in the state, wrote Langford about the need for legislation to prevent pot hunting. Langford, capable of viewing things from both the collectors' and scientists' viewpoints, felt that both landowners and amateur diggers needed to be treated with respect: "The average amateur who takes the trouble to dig is eager for information and quite amenable to reason unless treated as one of an unfavorable class intruding upon scientific perogatives [sic]." His suggested legislation would have allowed anyone to dig, upon securing a permit, would have included paleontological excavations, would have required monthly reports, and significantly, given Lanford's pioneering salvage work, would have called for "an accounting of accidental finds made during industrial, agricultural or other operations."[33]

The presence of Langford's collections at the University of Chicago eventually led to their use in several important studies.[34] James B. Griffin's study of the Fort Ancient Aspect made important use of the Fisher site materials. Early on, Kidder had seen the similarity of the Fisher site materials to that of Madisonville in Ohio,[35] although Langford used the term "Iroquoian" for the Middle Level (Griffin 1943: 268–272 provides a history of the classification of the Fisher materials). The Fisher ceramics were a major focus of Griffin's work and several other studies. Langford had divided the pottery from the site by temper (grit and shell), decoration, and surface treatment (Langford 1928a: 54). Later, James A. Ford examined the Fisher collection at the University of Michigan's ceramic repository and made a similar division that was used by Griffin.[36]

An issue of significance at the Fisher site was whether the grit- and shell-tempered pottery was used by different cultures or was contemporaneous. Langford's mound excavations suggested that shell-tempered pottery preceded the grit-tempered. The "holes" that dotted the site were a source of additional information on this question. A hole on the rim of Pit 8 was 4 feet deep and filled with refuse. In it were about three-quarters grit-tempered sherds and one-quarter shell-tempered. When he examined the artifacts he found that some of the grit-tempered sherds fit together, whereas none of the shell-tempered ones did. Also, the shell-tempered sherds were more weathered and worn. From this evidence he concluded that a later refuse pit of grit-tempered pottery users intruded into an older layer having shell-tempered pottery (Langford 1928a: 20–21).

Although the idea developed in the Southwest of giving binomial names to pottery types was introduced to the eastern United States in the 1930s (Griffin 1976: 25–26), it remained for John W. Griffin to actually name the Fisher site types. He used *Fisher* for the shell-tempered series of types and *Langford* for the grit-tempered series (Griffin 1946: 13–20). Later work in the upper Illinois River Valley led Brown (1961: 75; 1967: 36) to suggest the name *Langford tradition* for the local expression of Upper Mississippian culture. The differences between Langford and Fisher pottery and traditions has become a major topic of research in the northern Illinois and Indiana area (Berres 2001; Doershuk 1988; Emerson 1999; Markman 1991: 78–87).

The lack of any mention of Langford in most historical summaries of eastern/midwestern archaeology is a significant gap. There is no mention of Langford's work in Guthe (1952), Brose (1973), Griffin (1976), or Willey and Sabloff (1993), nor in any of the recent spate of articles on the "stratigraphic revolution" in American archaeology (Browman and Givens 1996; Lyman et al. 1997; Lyman and O'Brien 1999; Stein 2000). Some recognition of his work is briefly provided in historical summaries of Illinois archaeology by Fowler (1985: 6–7) and Muller (2002: 102), and Kullen (2000) has recently contributed to making Langford and his work better known to archaeologists.

Likewise, Langford's osteometric work on the Fisher skeletons has been ignored in summaries of midwestern physical anthropology (Buikstra 1979; Neumann 1952), as it was pretty much by his contemporaries. This later phenomenon may relate in part to archaeologists not knowing what exactly to do with such interpretations (Buikstra 1979: 221), although some of Langford's correspondents (Dixon, MacCurdy) were familiar with the issues of craniometry and racial interpretations. Racial classification of skeletal remains was standard practice at the time and continued at least into the 1950s, when there was a slow shift to population comparisons, rather than racial typology (Armelagos et al. 1982). Even so, the cranial data that Langford published is still useful for certain questions (Jamison 1971: 130).

One important exception to this general neglect of Langford's work is in Carl Guthe's review of the founding of the Society for American Archaeology, in which he makes the following observation about the state of archaeology in the Eastern U. S. in 1927: "The doubts which some archaeologists had about the existence of true stratigraphy in the area were dispelled forever by Langford's report in that year on his discoveries at the Fisher site in Illinois" (Guthe 1967: 434).[37]

Fisher after Langford

When Langford completed his work at the site in 1929, the site was owned by a gravel company that intended to quarry the area. For whatever reason, in 1940, much of the site still remained, and a joint Illinois State Museum and University of Chicago expedition directed by Gretchen Cutter and Winslow Walker and using WPA labor excavated at the site for nine months (Deuel 1940). Out of these operations came two University of Chicago master's theses, one on the Upper Mississippian occupation by John W. Griffin (1944, 1946, 1948) and one on the Late Woodland occupation by Charles E. Gillette (1949a, 1949b).

In 1946, Wheaton College sent a crew to the site to excavate a house pit in the northwest portion (Horner 1947). The author of the article on the work predicted that the site would disappear in the next five years through sand and gravel removal. It is unclear when this prophecy was confirmed, but the bulk of the site no longer exists (D. Kullen, pers. comm., 2000; J. A. Brown, pers. comm., 2002).

Langford after Fisher

The year after finishing work at Fisher, Langford was at work at the Adler mounds, sometimes with a field party from the University of Chicago. This excavation was referred to in articles (Eggan 1933; Krogman 1931) but was not written up until much later by Howard Winters, who praised Langford's work highly (Winters 1961). When the Adler excavation was completed, he donated his collections from that site and the Fisher site to the University of Chicago (Kullen 2000).

In the mid-1930s, Langford was still corresponding with Fay-Cooper Cole about a potentially promising site south of Joliet, and with Warren Moorehead concerning a report Moorehead was putting together with A. R. Kelly.[38] Although he had apparently given up active digging about this time, he never gave up thinking about archaeology and prehistoric people. In 1937, in the guise of "The Man of Chelles," Langford sent to the Patent Office an application for a stone scraper (Langford 1937a, 1955), illustrated in his own hand (as were his own patent applications, which numbered around 100). Much later, he returned to write his fourth children's book with a prehistoric theme (Langford 1954). Near the end of his life, he wrote a manuscript summarizing his archaeological explorations between 1898 to 1930 (Langford 1961).

Not one to sit by idly, in 1937 Langford took up paleobotany with a passion, although he had been collecting vertebrate fossils for many years. Fairly shortly, he and his son were donating significant collections to the Illinois State Museum (Leary 1996). By the late 1940s, he was living in Chicago and hotly pursuing fossil plants across the United States for the Chicago Natural History Museum (now Field Museum), of which he became curator of fossil plants in 1950. Near the end of his life he published guides to the Wilmington coal flora and fauna (better known as Mazon Creek), illustrated by his own photographs and drawings (Langford 1958, 1963). In his later years, he encountered in paleontology something that he had not in archaeology: resistance to his work from professionals because of his lack of training.[39]

Langford retired from the Field Museum in 1962 at the age of 86 and died two years later.

Conclusions

Although an amateur archaeologist by both his own definition and that of his contemporaries, Langford had much going for him that most of his fellow amateurs did not. As a professional engineer, he had the ability to record and communicate his findings to others. He was extremely adept at technical drawing, as well as illustrating his interpretations of the archaeological record, he could take and print publishable photographs, and he could produce museum-quality sculptures of prehistoric people and animals. By the time the Fisher site excavation started, Langford had three books for young adults in print, illustrated mostly with his own drawings, and one article in the principal American anthropological journal. As a Yale graduate, he had an automatic connection with faculty and staff there. His donations and sale of paleontological collections to major museums gave him recognition and access to those institutions. As a result of many of these factors he had the attention and respect of the archaeological community.

In a review of the origins of the Society for American Archaeology,

Guthe (1967: 434) points out that the 1920s was a period when amateur archaeology was seen by some professionals as "getting out of hand"; some felt that attempts should be made to increase contact between amateurs and professionals. One effort in this direction was establishment of the Committee on State Archaeological Surveys of the National Research Council, created to promote archaeological survey in several midwestern states by governmental and learned organizations in close cooperation with amateurs (Guthe 1930: 55). Nevertheless, at the end of the decade, Guthe (1967: 435) felt that "lack of communication between groups was enormous," particularly between archaeologists in different states and between professionals and laymen.

Clearly, Langford's experiences in promoting the Fisher site and his interpretations run counter to this general situation, and it was the Committee on State Archaeological Surveys that appears to have provided some of the structure for his interactions with American archaeologists. Most of the major archaeological contacts that he had during his excavation of the Fisher site were with chairmen or members of the committee (Kidder's correspondence was on National Research Council letterhead). Additional work needs to be done to determine to what extent the committee served to connect other amateur archaeologists with professionals (this topic is addressed somewhat in the introduction to O'Brien and Lyman 2001).

Langford's work was in many ways extraordinary, as was the man himself, and although frequently ignored in histories of midwestern archaeology, it served as an important basis for archaeological work in Illinois in the 1930s and later. The relationship of amateurs and professionals has never been a one-way street, and Langford is only one example of an amateur who helped in "setting the agenda for American archaeology," to use the title of a recent volume (O'Brien and Lyman 2001). It is fitting that Langford seems to have the distinction of being the only archaeologist in North America to have both a ceramic series and a cultural tradition named after him.[40]

Author's Note

I would like to thank Loren Kallsen for conducting preliminary research for me at the Minnesota Historical Society, Doug Kullen for sending me a pre-publication copy of his paper on Langford, and Doug Givens for providing copies of early *Teocentli* issues. The staffs of the Laboratory of Anthropology, University of Illinois at Urbana-Champaign, and the Minnesota Historical Society assisted me when I was conducting research in their archives. I also appreciate the assistance of Jim Konecny, who worked with Langford on his final publication and provided useful information on Langford's paleobotany work. I had the good fortune to audit a seminar on "The History and Theory of World Archaeology" given by the late James B. Griffin at UCLA in 1977. My notes from the lectures and from individual discussions with him helped me fill out some of the details on the University of Chicago's archaeological program and the state of midwestern archaeology in the late 1920s.

Notes

1. Page numbers in Langford (n.d.a) are my own.

2. The University of Chicago gave the designations $Wi°5$, 7–12 to the mounds and Wi^v6 to the village.

3. Langford had close contact with paleontologists Henry Fairfield Osborn and Walter Granger between 1909 and 1925 (notes in the George Langford Papers, Box 2, Minnesota Historical Society, St. Paul, hereafter cited as Langford Papers). Osborn wrote an introduction to Langford's first children's book (Langford 1920). Langford also knew and corresponded with Barnum Brown. Brown, who was closely involved in the search for evidence of early humans in North America, was called to the Folsom site in 1927 to view a fluted point in place next to the ribs of an extinct bison; in turn, he telegraphed museums and scholars to come out and see the "arrows [sic]" (Folsom 1974: 38–39). In Langford's papers at the Minnesota Historical Society is a telegram that Brown sent him requesting his presence at the site to view the find. Clearly, Langford's connections as an amateur paleontologist were as strong as those he had as an amateur archaeologist.

4. Berthold Laufer of the museum was, however, on the subcommittee for Illinois of the Committee on State Archaeological Surveys, National Research Council (Guthe 1930: 52), and that indicates at least a minimal interest in local archaeology. Illinois had a long history of lack of institutional interest in archaeology of the state (see Snyder 1899; 1900: 28–29). In a letter to Langford, W. K. Moorehead wrote of trying for many years with no result to interest the Field Museum in Illinois archaeology. Moorehead to Langford, December 18, 1929, Laboratory of Anthropology, University of Illinois, Urbana-Champaign (hereafter cited as Laboratory of Anthropology).

5. George Grant MacCurdy to Langford, May 21, 1919, and Henry Fairfield Osborn to Langford, February 10, 1919, both in Langford Papers, Box 1.

6. David Kinley to Langford, January 13, 1922, Langford Papers, Box 1.

7. N. C. Nelson to Langford, February 2, 1925, Illinois State Museum, Springfield.

8. See note 4.

9. Ohio was considered to be the best place to learn field techniques in the 1920s (J. B. Griffin, pers. comm, January 27, 1977).

10. George Grant MacCurdy to Langford, April 11, 1925, Langford Papers, Box 1.

11. George Grant MacCurdy to Langford, December 8, 1925, ibid.

12. Robert Lowie to Langford, March 31, 1926, ibid.

13. Roland B. Dixon to Langford, March 30, 1926, ibid.

14. Clark Wissler to Langford, April 14, 1919, ibid.

15. Clark Wissler to Langford, April 19, 1926, ibid.

16. A. V. Kidder to Langford, October 20, 1926, ibid.

17. Ibid.

18. A. V. Kidder to Langford, March 12, 1927, ibid.

19. A. V. Kidder to Langford, April 2, 1927, ibid.

20. According to Jesse Jennings (1994: 44), attendance at the summer archaeological field school was mandatory for all anthropology graduate students in 1931, and this rule was still in force in 1938 and 1939 (Spicer 1990: 14).

21. Langford to F.-C. Cole, August 19, 1926, Laboratory of Anthropology.

22. F.-C. Cole to Langford, May 23, 26, 1927, Langford Papers, Box 1.

23. Langford to F.-C. Cole, May 31, 1927, ibid.

24. F.-C. Cole to Langford, June 14, 1927, ibid.

25. F.-C. Cole to Langford, September 15, 1927, ibid. Kidder's diaries from the 1920s are not available to determine whether or not he came to Chicago at that time.

26. F.-C. Cole to Langford, January 6, 1928, ibid.

27. J. Maulds to Langford, January 24, 1930, ibid.

28. Frank Thone to Langford, December 23, 1926, ibid.

29. Langford to F.-C. Cole, February 15, 1929, Papers of the Department of Anthropology, Box 8, Folder 8, University of Chicago, Joseph Regenstein Library, Special Collections (hereafter cited as Papers of the Department of Anthropology).

30. Further evidence of the strong connectivity of American archaeology, suggested by Browman and Givens (1996: 91) for the previous decade.

31. James B. Griffin, a student of Cole's, said that the first time he read Kidder's *Introduction* was when he went to Michigan in 1933 (pers. comm., January 27, 1977). Carl Guthe, an assistant to Kidder at Pecos, was at Michigan at that time.

32. I do not know how to interpret Jimmy Griffin's comments to me that in the period 1929 to 1930 or 1931, Cole did not believe that there was stratigraphy in Illinois (pers. comm., January 27, 1977). At that time, Cole had been working with and supporting Langford for at least two years, and nothing in his letters indicates that he doubted Langford's stratigraphic observations. Referring to the eastern United States, Moorehead (1929a: 553) claimed that "we can not establish stratigraphy as at Pecos," even though he had just cited Langford's work three pages earlier.

33. Langford to W. K. Moorehead, October 3, 1928, Langford Papers, Box 1.

34. When Cole retired in 1947, the Illinois archaeology program that he had developed was basically eliminated (MacNeish 1998: 62), and the collections that he and his students had made in the previous two decades were broken up, with the Langford materials going mostly to the University of Illinois. Jimmy Griffin was still justifiably mad about this event thirty years later (pers. comm., January 20, 1977).

35. A. V. Kidder to Langford, April 2, 1927, Langford Papers, Box 1.

36. Gretchen Cutter was in charge of the 1940 excavations at Fisher, wrote a manuscript on the pottery, and was apparently planning a definitive report on the site (Griffin 1943: 283n. 34).

37. Although not a founding member of the SAA, Langford was a member in 1936–37 and was nominated to be a fellow in 1939 (Carl Guthe to Langford, May 12, Papers of the Department of Anthropology).

38. November 8, 1934, Laboratory of Anthropology; W. K. Moorehead to Langford, October 21, 1936, ibid.

39. George Langford Jr. to Don Auler, December 1986, copy in possession of the author.

40. The Titterington phase, named after St. Louis amateur Paul Titterington, and the Schultz Phase, named after Kansas amateur Floyd Schultz, are other examples of archaeological entities in the Midwest that were named for archaeologists.

References

"Amateurs in Field of Science Performing Remarkable Work." 1926. Science Service article from unknown newspaper. George Langford Papers, Box 1, Minnesota Historical Society, St. Paul.

Armelagos, G. J., D. S. Carlson, and D. P. Van Gerven. 1982. "The Theoretical Foundations and Development of Skeletal Biology." In *A History of American Physical Anthropology, 1930–1980,* edited by F. Spencer, 305–328. New York: Academic Press.

Baerreis, D. A., E. Wheeler-Voegelin, and R. Wycoco-Moore. 1974. "Anthropological Report on the Chippewa, Ottawa, and Potawatomi Indians of Royce Area 148." In *Indians of Northeastern Illinois,* 51–246. American Indian Ethnohistory series. New York: Garland Publishing.

Bennett, J. W. 1945. *Archaeological Explorations in Jo Daviess County, Illinois: The Work of William Baker Nickerson (1895–1901) and the University of Chicago (1926–32).* Chicago: University of Chicago Press.

Bentley, M. 1931. *In Quest of Glacial Man: A Plan of Cooperation Between Excavators and the Representatives of the Sciences of Man and of the Earth.* Reprint and Circular Series of the National Research Council no. 100.

Berres, T. E. 2001. *Power and Gender in Oneota Culture: A Study of a Late Prehistoric People*. DeKalb: Northern Illinois University Press.

Black, G. A. 1961. "that what is past may not be forever lost . . ." *Indiana History Bulletin* 38 (4): 51–69.

Brose, D. S. 1973. "The Northeastern United States." In *The Development of North American Archaeology*, edited by J. E. Fitting, 84–115. New York: Anchor Books.

Browman, D. L. 2002. "Origins of Stratigraphic Excavation in North America: The Peabody Museum Method and the Chicago Method." In *New Perspectives on the Origins of Americanist Archaeology*, edited by D. L. Browman and S. Williams, 242–264. Tuscaloosa: University of Alabama Press.

Browman, D. L., and D. R. Givens. 1996. "Stratigraphic Excavation: The First 'New Archaeology.'" *American Anthropologist* 98: 80–95.

Brown, J. A. 1961. *The Zimmerman Site: A Report on Excavations at the Grand Village of Kaskaskia, LaSalle County, Illinois*. Illinois State Museum Report of Investigations no. 9.

———. 1967. *The Gentleman Farm Site, LaSalle County, Illinois*. Illinois State Museum Reports of Investigations no. 12.

Buikstra, J. 1979. "Contributions of Physical Anthropologists to the Concept of Hopewell: A Historical Perspective." In *Hopewell Archaeology: The Chillicothe Conference*, edited by D. S. Brose and N. Greber, 220–233. Kent, Ohio: Kent State University Press.

Cole, F.-C. 1932. "Exploration and Excavation." In *Conference on Southern Prehistory*, 74–78. Washington, D.C.: National Research Council.

———. 1935. "Letter." In *The Indianapolis Conference: A Symposium upon the Archaeological Problems of the North Central United States Area*, 39–43. Washington, D.C.: Committee on State Archaeological Surveys, Division of Anthropology and Psychology, National Research Council.

———. 1936. "Prehistoric Archaeology." A lecture given before the Division of Social Sciences, University of Chicago, November 3. Copy in Papers of the Department of Anthropology, Box 2, Folder 8, Department of Special Collections, University of Chicago Library.

Cole, F.-C., and T. Deuel. 1931. "Rediscovering Illinois." In *Blue Book of the State of Illinois, 1931–1932*, edited by W. J. Stratton, 318–341. Springfield: State of Illinois.

———. 1937. *Rediscovering Illinois: Archaeological Explorations in and around Fulton County*. Chicago: University of Chicago Press.

Deuel, T. 1940. "Archaeological Field Work of the Illinois State Museum, Springfield, Ill." *Quarterly Bulletin of the Illinois State Archaeological Society* 3 (1): 3–7.

Dixon, R. B. 1923. *The Racial History of Man*. New York: Scribners.

Doershuk, J. 1988. *Plenemuk Mound and the Archaeology of Will County, Illinois*. Illinois Historic Preservation Agency Cultural Resource Study 3.

"Earthworks Tell of Early Americans." 1928. *Science News-Letter*, May 19, 1928, 309.

Eggan, F. 1933. "The Archaeology of Will County." *Transactions of the Illinois State Academy of Science* 25 (4): 93–95.

———. 1974. "Among the Anthropologists." *Annual Review of Anthropology* 3: 1–19.

Emerson, T. E. 1999. "The Langford Tradition and the Process of Tribalization on the Middle Mississippian Borders." *Mid-Continental Journal of Archaeology* 24: 3–56.

Folsom, F. 1974. "An Amateur's Bonanza: Discovery of Early Man in North America." *American West* 11 (6): 34–39.

Fowler, M. L. 1962. "An Appraisal." In *John Francis Snyder: Selected Writings*, edited by C. C. Walton, 181–189. Springfield: Illinois State Historical Society.

———. 1985. *A Brief History of Illinois Archaeology*. Illinois Archaeological Survey Bulletin 1: 3–11.

Gillette, C. E. 1949a. "The Non-Mississippian Manifestations at the Fisher Site, Will County, Illinois." Master's thesis, University of Chicago.

———. 1949b. "Late Woodland Occupations of the Fisher Site, Will County, Illinois." *Illinois Academy of Science Transactions* 42: 35–40.

Greenman, E. F. 1929. "A Form for Collection Inventories." In *Report of the Conference on Midwestern Archaeology, Held in St. Louis, Missouri, May 18, 1929*, 82–86. Bulletin of the National Research Council no. 74.

Griffin, J. B. 1943. *The Fort Ancient Aspect, Its Cultural and Chronological Position in Mississippi Valley Archaeology*. Anthropological Papers no. 28. Museum of Anthropology, University of Michigan.

———. 1976. "A Commentary on Some Archaeological Activities in the Mid-Continent 1925–1975." *Mid-Continental Journal of Archaeology* 1: 5–38.

Griffin, J. W. 1944. "New Evidence from the Fisher Site." *Illinois Academy of Science Transactions* 37: 37–40.

———. 1946. "The Upper Mississippi Occupations of the Fisher Site, Will County, Illinois." Master's thesis, University of Chicago.

———. 1948. "Upper Mississippi at the Fisher Site." *American Antiquity* 14: 124–126.

Guthe, C. E. 1928. "Report of the Chairman on a Trip Through the Mississippi Valley, September 1928." Committee on State Archaeological Surveys. Papers of the Department of Anthropology, Box 8, Folder 8, Special Collections, Joseph Regenstein Library, University of Chicago.

———. 1930. "The Committee on State Archaeological Surveys in the Division of Anthropology and Psychology, National Research Council." In *Proceedings of the Twenty-Third International Congress of Americanists*, 52–59. New York.

———. 1952. "Twenty-five Years of Archeology in the Eastern United States." In *Archeology of the Eastern United States*, edited by J. B. Griffin, 1–12. Chicago: University of Chicago Press.

———. 1967. "Reflections on the Founding of the Society for American Archaeology." *American Antiquity* 32: 433–440.

Haag, W. G. 1986. "Field Methods in Archaeology." In *American Archaeology: Past and Future*, edited by D. J. Meltzer, D. D. Fowler, and J. A. Sabloff, 63–76. Washington, D.C.: Smithsonian Institution Press.

Harris, E. 1982. *Principles of Archaeological Stratigraphy.* 2d ed. London: Academic Press.

Homsher, G. W. 1884. "The Glid[e]well Mound, Franklin County, Indiana." *Annual Report of the Smithsonian Institution for 1882*, 721–728. Washington, D.C.: Government Printing Office.

Horner, G. R. 1947. "An Upper-Mississippi House-Pit from the Fisher Village Site: Further Evidence." *Illinois Academy of Science Transactions* 40: 26–29.

Hrdlička, A. 1920. *Anthropometry.* Philadelphia: Wistar Institute.

Hull, D. L. 2002. "Prematurity and Promise: Why Was Stent's Notion of Prematurity Itself So Premature?" In *Prematurity in Scientific Discovery: On Resistance and Neglect*, edited by E. B. Hook, 329–341. Berkeley and Los Angeles: University of California Press.

"Indian Mounds of Illinois." 1926. *Science* 64 (supplement 1670): xii.

Jamison, P. L. 1971. "A Demographic and Comparative Analysis of the Albany Mounds (Illinois) Hopewell Skeletons." In *The Indian Mounds at Albany, Illinois*, edited by E. B. Herold, 107–153. Davenport Museum Anthropological Papers no. 1.

Jennings, J. D. 1994. *Accidental Archaeologist.* Salt Lake City: University of Utah Press.

Jones, V. H. 1976. "James Bennett Griffin, Archaeologist." In *Cultural Change and Continuity: Essays in Honor of James Bennett Griffin*, edited by C. E. Cleland, xxxix–lxxvii. New York: Academic Press.

Kelly, J. E. 2000. "Introduction." In *The Cahokia Mounds*, by W. K. Moorehead, 1–57. Tuscaloosa: University of Alabama Press.

Kidder, A. V. 1927. Letter. *Teocentli* 4: 6.

Krogman, W. M. 1927. "Notes on the Fisher Site." On file at Laboratory of Anthropology, University of Illinois at Urbana-Champaign.

———. 1931. "The Archaeology of the Chicago Area." *Transactions of the Illinois State Academy of Science* 23: 413–420.

Kullen, D. 2000. "Reminiscences of George Langford." *Illinois Archaeology* 12: 110–124.

Langford, G. 1919. "The Kankakee River Refuse Heap: Evidence of a Unique and Primitive Culture in the Southwestern Chicago Area." *American Anthropologist* 21: 287–291.

———. 1920. *Pic, the Weapon Maker.* New York: Boni and Liveright.

———. 1923. *Stories of the First American Mammals.* New York: Boni and Liveright.

———. 1927. "The Fisher Mound Group, Successive Aboriginal Occupations near the Mouth of the Illinois River." *American Anthropologist* 29: 153–205.

———. 1928a. "The Fisher Site: Exploration of the Pits." Typed report at Laboratory of Anthropology, University of Illinois at Urbana-Champaign.

———. 1928b. "Stratified Indian Mounds in Will County." *Illinois State Academy of Science, Transactions* 20: 247–253.

———. 1929. "The Fisher Site: Exploration of the Pits." *Illinois State Academy of Science, Transactions* 22: 79–92.

———. 1930a. "Work Done in 1928 Upon the Fisher Site." Manuscript at the Laboratory of Anthropology, University of Illinois, Urbana-Champaign.

———. 1930b. "Work Done in 1929 Upon the Fisher Site." Manuscript at the Laboratory of Anthropology, University of Illinois, Urbana-Champaign.

———. 1930c. "Fisher's, Book IV—The Two Big Mounds." Field notes on file at the Laboratory of Anthropology, University of Illinois, Urbana-Champaign.

———. 1930d. "Fisher's, Book V—The Pits." Field notes on file at the Laboratory of Anthropology, University of Illinois, Urbana-Champaign.

———. 1937a. "Paleolithic Patent No. 1—Stone Tool." *Journal of the Patent Office Society* 19: 346–358.

———. 1937b. "Chipped Stone Projectile Points. As Told by a Neolithic Flint-Worker 10,000 Years B.C." Handprinted manuscript. Illinois State Museum, Springfield.

———. 1954. *Senrac, the Lion Man.* New York: Liveright.

———. 1955. "Patent Applied for—on 250,000-Year-Old Invention." *Chicago Natural History Museum Bulletin,* August, 3.

———. 1958. *The Wilmington Coal Flora from a Pennsylvanian Deposit in Will County, Illinois.* Downers Grove, Ill.: Esconi Associates.

———. 1961. "Prehistory of the Chicago Region, 800–1800 A.D." Handwritten manuscript. George Langford Papers, Minnesota Historical Society, St. Paul.

———. 1963. *The Wilmington Coal Fauna and Additions to the Wilmington Coal Flora from a Pennsylvanian Deposit in Will County, Illinois.* Downers Grove, Ill.: Esconi Associates.

———. 2001. Diary. Edited by Jim and Sylvia Konecny. Privately distributed.

———. n.d.a. "The Fisher Site." Manuscript on file at the Illinois State Museum, Springfield.

———. n.d.b. "The Fisher Indian Mound and Village Site." Manuscript. Papers of George Langford, Box 3, Vol. 19, Minnesota Historical Society, St. Paul.

"Langford to Tell Scientists of Prehistoric Men." 1927. *Spectator,* April 22, 1927.

Leary, R. L. 1996. "George Langford, Sr. (1876–1964): Amateur Paleobotanist and Inventor." *Living Museum* 58 (2–3): 36–38.

Leighton, M. M. 1923. "The Geological Aspects of Some of the Cahokia (Illinois) Mounds." In *The Cahokia Mounds.* University of Illinois Bulletin 21 (6): 109–143.

Lyman, R. L., and M. J. O'Brien. 1999. "Americanist Stratigraphic Excavation and the Measurement of Culture Change." *Journal of Archaeological Method and Theory* 6: 55–108.

Lyman, R. L., M. J. O'Brien, and R. C. Dunnell. 1997. *The Rise and Fall of Culture History.* New York: Plenum.

MacCurdy, G. G. 1924. *Human Origins: A Manual of Prehistory.* New York: Appleton.

MacNeish, R. S. 1998. "My Life in Canadian Archaeology." In *Bringing Back the Past: Historical Perspectives on Canadian Archaeology,* edited by P. J. Smith and D. Mitchell, 61–76. Archaeological Survey of Canada Mercury Series Paper 158.

Markman, C. W. 1991. *Chicago Before History: The Prehistoric Archaeology of a Modern Metropolitan Area.* Illinois Historic Preservation Agency Studies in Illinois Archaeology 7.

McGimsey, C. R., III. 1998. "Teocentli: A Brief Introduction." In *Gleanings from the First Fifty Years of Teocentli,* edited by C. R. McGimsey II, v–vi. Occasional Papers no. 1, Bulletin of the History of Archaeology.

Mills, W. C. 1902. "Excavation of the Adena Mound." *Ohio Archaeological and Historical Society Publications* 10: 452–479.

Moorehead, W. K. 1929a. "The Mound Builder Problem to Date." *American Anthropologist* 31: 5449–5554.

———. 1929b. *The Cahokia Mounds.* University of Illinois Bulletin 26 (4).

———. 1930a. "Prehistoric Cultural Areas East of the Rocky Mountains." In *Proceedings of the Twenty-Third International Congress of Americanists,* 47–51. New York.

———. 1930b. "Cultural Affinities and Differences in Illinois Archaeology." *Transactions of the Illinois State Academy of Science* 22: 23–40.

Muller, J. 2002. "Rediscovering Illinois: The Development of Archaeology in Illinois." In *Histories of Southeastern Archaeology,* edited by S. Tushingham, J. Hill, and C. H. McNutt, 99–114. Tuscaloosa: University of Alabama Press.

Nash, S. E. 1999. *Time, Trees, and Prehistory: Tree-Ring Dating and the Development of North American Archaeology, 1914 to 1950.* Salt Lake City: University of Utah Press.

National Research Council. 1930. *Guide Leaflet for Amateur Archaeologists.* Reprint and Circular Series no. 93.

Neitzel, R. S. 1994. "Culture, Beigabe, and History." In *Pioneers in Historical Archaeology: Breaking New Ground,* edited by S. South, 125–163. New York: Plenum.

Neumann, G. K. 1952. "Archeology and Race in the American Indian." In *Archeology of Eastern United States,* edited by J. B. Griffin, 13–34. Chicago: University of Chicago Press.

Nickerson, W. B. 1908. "Mounds of Northwestern Illinois." *Records of the Past* 7: 85–95.

————. 1912. "The Burial Mounds at Albany, Illinois." *Records of the Past* 11: 69–81.

O'Brien, M. J. 1996. *Paradigms of the Past: The Story of Missouri Archaeology.* Columbia: University of Missouri Press.

O'Brien, M. J., and R. L. Lyman, eds. 2001. *Setting the Agenda for American Archaeology: The National Research Council Archaeological Conferences of 1929, 1932, and 1935.* Tuscaloosa: University of Alabama Press.

Parmalee, P. K. 1962. "The Faunal Complex of the Fisher Site, Illinois." *American Midland Naturalist* 68: 399–408.

Putnam, F. W. 1882. "Archaeological Explorations at Madisonville, Ohio." *Fifteenth Annual Report, Peabody Museum of Archaeology and Ethnology, Harvard University,* 62–67.

————. 1883. "Archaeological Explorations at Madisonville and Other Sites in the Little Miami River Valley, Ohio." *Sixteenth Annual Report, Peabody Museum of Archaeology and Ethnology, Harvard University,* 165–176.

"Recent Mound-Builders." 1928. *Literary Digest,* October 6.

Rowe, J. H. 1975. Review of *A History of American Archaeology,* by Gordon R. Willey and Jeremy A. Sabloff. *Antiquity* 49: 156–158.

Schnapp, A. 1997. *The Discovery of the Past.* New York: Harry N. Abrams.

Shetrone, H. C. 1920. "The Culture Problem in Ohio Archaeology." *American Anthropologist* 22: 144–172.

————. 1930 [1941]. *The Mound-Builders.* New York: D. Appleton-Century.

Snead, J. E. 2001. *Ruins and Rivals: The Making of Southwest Archaeology.* Tucson: University of Arizona Press.

Snyder, J. F. 1899. Editorial. *The American Archaeologist* 2: 191–192.

————. 1900. "The Field for Archaeological Research in Illinois." *Transactions of the Illinois State Historical Society for 1900,* 21–29.

Spicer, R. B. 1990. "A Full Life Well Lived: A Brief Account of the Life of Edward H. Spicer." *Journal of the Southwest* 32 (1): 3–17.

"State History Society Opens Sessions Here." 1929. *Joliet Evening Herald,* October 30.

Stein, J. K. 2000. "Stratigraphy and Archaeological Dating." In *It's About Time: A History of Archaeological Dating in North America,* edited by S. E. Nash, 14–40. Salt Lake City: University of Utah Press.

Stocking, G. W., Jr. 1979. "Interview and Department Focus: George Stocking on Fay-Cooper Cole." *Journal of Anthropology* 1 (2): 1–17.

"St. Paul Boy's Hobby Leads to Discovery of 7 Lost Races of American Indians." 1930. *Minneapolis Journal,* April 20.

Thone, F. 1926. "Indian City of the Dead Found in Illinois." *Science News-Letter* 10 (296): 161–162, 167.

Ward, D.J.H. 1905. "The Investigation of the Okoboji Mounds and the Finds." *Iowa Journal of History and Politics* 3: 427–435.

Willey, G. R., and J. A. Sabloff. 1993. *A History of American Archaeology.* 3d ed. New York: W. H. Freeman.

Winters, H. D. 1961. "The Adler Mound Group, Will County, Illinois." In *Chicago Area Archaeology,* edited by E. A. Bluhm, 57–88. Illinois Archaeological Survey Bulletin 3.

Wissler, C. 1917. "The 'New' American Archaeology." *American Museum Journal* 17: 100–101.

———. 1922. *The American Indian.* New York: D. C. McMurtrie.

Wray, D. E. 1952. "Archeology of the Illinois Valley: 1950." In *Archeology of the Eastern United States,* edited by J. B. Griffin, 152–164. Chicago: University of Chicago Press.

Zuckerman, H., and J. Lederberg. 1986. "Postmature Scientific Discovery?" *Nature* 324: 629–631.

8

Not So Talkative Tree Rings

Why Did Archaeologists Wait for an Astronomer
to Establish Tree-Ring Dating?

Stephen E. Nash

In the December 1929 issue of *Natural Geographic Magazine*, Andrew
Ellicott Douglass of the University of Arizona published an article titled
"The Secret of the Southwest Solved by Talkative Tree-Rings." This seminal contribution presented, for the first time, Christian calendar dates for
the construction and occupation of some 40 prehistoric pueblos on the
Colorado Plateau. Prior to this publication, archaeologists working in the
American Southwest had literally no realistic idea of how old the prehistoric ruins were (Haury 1995; Zeuner 1951). Educated guesses suggested
that ruins such as Pecos Pueblo might be 1,000 or 1,500 years old (Kidder
1927, 1936), and that Basketmaker occupations in the San Juan region
might be between 3,000 and 4,000 years old (see Baldwin 1938; Cornelius
1938; Kidder 1924; Renaud 1928; Roberts 1935, 1937). The most immediate effects of tree-ring dating on archaeological interpretation was that
it collapsed, by about 50 percent, the guesstimated age of the prehistoric
pueblos. In addition, the guesstimated time of construction, occupation,
and abandonment of massive stone apartment buildings like Pueblo Bonito was cut from centuries to decades.

Archaeologists were astonished at how young the classic southwestern
sites actually were. Because tree-ring dates compressed, rather than tele-
scoped, their age estimates, archaeologists were forced to revise their interpretations of prehistoric occupations of the Southwest. As a result, archaeologists such as Earl Halstead Morris and Alfred Vincent Kidder were
disappointed: "[We] have a sneaking sense of disappointment as the piti-
less progress of tree-ring dating hauls the Cliff-dwellers, and with them the
Basketmakers, farther and farther away from the cherished B.C.'s" (Kid-

der 1936: 143). The impact of absolute chronology and the compressed timetable on archaeological interpretation is perhaps best conveyed in the words of an eyewitness, Emil Walter Haury:

We found the Southwestern timetable sorely in error once tree-time became applicable. As an example, we have the estimates of the mid-1920's for the Basketmakers, the earliest members of what we now call [the] Anasazi, which dated [prior to tree-ring dating at] some 2000 B.C. This was patently an inferred date based on the assumption that cultural progress in the region was slow. Later, with the application of tree-time, and as Basketmaker sites were demonstrably shown to have been inhabited during the early centuries of the Christian era, this figure was cut in half. At once, this threw entirely new light on the rapidity of culture growth, that instead of the slow, measured progress, changes in the Southwest were effected rapidly. The 500-room pueblo of the twelfth century assumed to have been to have been the end product of innumerable centuries of tedious groping for better homes, rooted in the individual semisubterranean house, could now be shown to have developed quickly, in the span of a few centuries. What thus appeared to be true of architecture was therefore also inherent in the growth of arts and crafts. (Haury 1946)

In 1935, Haury wrote, "It may be stated without equivocation that the tree-ring approach has been the single greatest contribution ever made to American archaeology" (98). Five decades later, dendrochronologists Bryant Bannister and William Robinson (1986: 51) stated, "The existence of a reliable chronological framework on which to chart the development of prehistoric cultures not only profoundly changed the structure of Southwestern investigations but also altered the thinking of all New World archaeologists." Even today, it would be difficult to overstate the impact of dendrochronology on the development of archaeological method and theory. Archaeologists were forced to revise their theories regarding rates of cultural evolution, site occupation duration, population densities, rates of population growth, rates of culture trait diffusion, and a host of other estimates on which the science of archaeology was based. Tree-ring dating also brought paleoenvironmental reconstruction to archaeologists' analytical repertoire and set the stage for studies of human ecology over the succeeding decades (Nash and Dean, in press).

From an institutional and educational perspective, graduate students flocked to learn the new science of dendrochronology. Within two years (by 1931) of Douglass's *National Geographic* publication, no fewer than four universities and museums had hired Douglass's students and established their own archaeological tree-ring dating programs. That these laboratories were established during the height of the Great Depression is testimony to the level of importance awarded tree-ring dating during this period. The economic predicament of the era is nothing short of astonishing: between 1929 and 1933, the gross national product of the United States dropped by 29 percent, investment dropped by 98 percent, construction spending dropped by 78 percent, and unemployment rose from roughly 3 to 25 percent (McElvaine 1993).

What is surprising in the developmental history of archaeological tree-ring dating is the indifference that many archaeologists had to the issue of archaeological dating prior to Douglass's publication. A select few archaeologists, including Morris, Kidder, Haury, Neil Merton Judd, Lyndon Lane Hargrave, and others, contributed greatly to the development of archaeological tree-ring dating in the 1920s, but during the preceding two decades (between ca. 1910 and the first Pecos Conference in 1927) (Kidder 1927), scarcely an archaeologist showed an interest in Douglass's work.

In this chapter, I will examine the earliest history of archaeological tree-ring dating, particularly events that occurred prior to 1920. It will become clear that, despite prior demonstrations of crossdating, the basic principle of dendrochronology, and several attempts by archaeologists to elucidate the age of ruins by counting tree rings, archaeologists simply did not capitalize on tree-ring dating until relatively late in its developmental trajectory. Indeed, in the absence of Clark Wissler's astute observation that Douglass's tree-ring method might work on prehistoric timbers in the Southwest, archaeological tree-ring dating may not have developed at all.

Archaeologists' Interest in Time

Though it is common knowledge that the study of artifacts and temporal relationships are what distinguish archaeology from the other subfields of anthropology, time remains the most recalcitrant dimension that archaeologists have to confront. The analysis of material culture is older than the discipline of archaeology itself and traces back to the earliest recognition of prehistoric artifacts in Europe (Daniel 1963). The study of time as represented in the archaeological record has a much shorter pedigree, however, and critical examination of published and unpublished documents reveals a rather astonishing lack of interest in time by archaeologists, especially prior to the second decade of the twentieth century (Chazan 1996; Dark 1995: 64; Nash 1999; Shanks and Tilley 1987: 118; contra Lyman et al. 1997).

American archaeology prior to 1914 focused almost exclusively on artifactual and architectural classification, description, and typology (Willey and Sabloff 1980). As archaeologists gained control over these realms, they began, slowly but surely, to examine temporal relationships in the archaeological record by experimenting with stratigraphic excavation techniques (Kidder 1924, 1958; Nelson 1916; see also Nelson 1918; Spier 1931) and serial analyses (Kroeber 1916; Spier 1917a, 1917b, 1931) developed by their European contemporaries and predecessors. Though these archaeologists made inferences regarding temporal relationships on the basis of these analyses, they were not "measuring" time in any real sense (contra Lyman et al. 1997). Marking sequences in the stratigraphic record they were; measuring time, they were not. In order to *measure* time, archaeologists need an absolute dating technique that is calibrated to some external calendar. Dendrochronology in the Douglass method provided the first calibrated calendar.

It is important to note that the stimulus to chronological research for North American archaeologists came not from within their own ranks but from their ethnological colleagues. Ethnologist Berthold Laufer of the Field Museum of Natural History in Chicago offered his understanding of the task at hand in a review of archaeologist Roland Dixon's (1913) "Some Aspects of North American Archaeology." Laufer wrote that "chronology is at the root of the matter, being the nerve electrifying the dead body of history. It should be incumbent upon the American archaeologist to establish a chronological basis of the pre-Columbian cultures, and the American ethnologist should make it a point to bring chronology into the life and history of the pre-Columbian Indians" (Laufer 1913: 577). Nearly a decade after Laufer's admonition, many North American archaeologists still did not share the interest in chronology already demonstrated by Alfred Kroeber, Nels Christian Nelson, and Leslie Spier. Clark Wissler of the American Museum of Natural History (AMNH) explained the situation to his colleague Sylvanus Morley as he described debate over the agenda for an archaeological conference to be held at Pueblo Bonito in Chaco Canyon, New Mexico:

Strange to say, there was among anthropologists in general a considerable indifference and even hostility to the chronological idea. With the waning of [Frederic Ward] Putnam's influence [see Meltzer

1985] this reaction gathered strength until the whole subject [of chronology] was taboo. The time was, a few years ago, when no one dared mention the fact that there might be important differences in our dates [sic; no absolute dates were yet available to archaeologists]. Happily the development of anthropology in Europe has brought us to our senses again. We must establish a chronology for the New World and acknowledge our incompetence. Without a true time perspective the data of our subject will be a chaos of facts from which the general reader and even the student will flee as from a pestilence (August 16, 1921).

As of about 1920, then, Kroeber, Spier, and Nelson were actively engaged in analyses that could inform chronological relationships in the archaeological record, but most archaeologists had not recognized the importance and implications of dating the archaeological record. Chronology (with a capital C), especially chronometry, was simply not on their conceptual radar screens. What, then, is tree-ring dating? It is crossdating, chronology construction, and comparative analysis. Why was it not on archaeologists' radar screens? It is based in natural, not social, science and was therefore largely out of the intellectual domain frequented by archaeologists interested in material culture and architecture. How did it come to be on their screens? In three phases, all of which of can be credited to Clark Wissler. The first began when Wissler, an ethnologist with training in psychology and an interest in culture-area and age-area theory, had a brilliant insight after reading Douglass's (1914) work. The second began in 1918, when Wissler first suggested that the relative tree-ring dating of archaeological sites, in this case Pueblo Bonito and Aztec Ruin, was a significant contribution in and of itself. The third began in 1921, when Wissler arranged for Neil Judd of the United States National Museum and the National Geographic Society to support Douglass's archaeological tree-ring work.

Crossdating

Dendrochronology, the study of tree time, is the highly specialized science of assigning Christian calendar dates to the growth rings of trees (Stokes and Smiley 1968). Tree-ring dates are the most accurate, precise, and therefore reliable chronometric data available to archaeologists (Dean 1978). We must be absolutely clear that tree-ring dating is *not* ring counting. To accurately determine Christian calendar dates for tree rings, the dendrochronologist must have intimate knowledge of the vagaries of ring growth found in trees in a given region. To gain this knowledge, he or she must visually compare and match the patterns of ring growth in large numbers of specimens from a single species. This fundamental practice, which has since been elevated to a principle of tree-ring dating, is called *crossdating* (Douglass 1941).

Crossdating is classically defined as "the procedure of matching ring width variations . . . among trees that have grown in nearby areas, allowing the identification of the exact year in which each ring formed" (Fritts 1976: 534). Note the emphasis on ring-width pattern matching, the absence of any suggestion of "ring-counting," and the implication that accurate tree-ring dating begins with the analysis of specimens from living trees. In the absence of accurate crossdating by the dendrochronologist, tree-ring specimens and chronologies cannot be considered accurately dated, and any interpretations that are predicated on those specimens or chronologies must be considered invalid (Baillie 1995).

From a dendrochronological perspective, all properly crossdated tree-ring dates are equal. There is no associated statistical uncertainty associated with properly crossdated tree-ring dates; a corollary is that tree-ring specimens either date or they do not. Responsible dendrochronologists do not succumb when archaeologists ask for a "likely date" (Baillie 1995).

The mechanics of crossdating are at once elegantly simple and maddeningly complex. As performed in the Douglass system, the dendrochronologist creates a graphic representation of the ring-width variability know as a *skeleton plot*, in which long lines are written on graph paper to indicate relatively narrow rings, a *B* is written to indicate a relatively large ring, and other unique attributes that may assist in the dating are noted directly on the plot (see Stokes and Smiley 1968). The skeleton plot is then compared to the master chronology, which is developed only after comparing the ring series in large numbers of trees from the same area or region. When the pattern indicated in the skeleton plot matches the pattern on the master chronology and all missing, double, or locally absent rings have been identified, an accurate and precise date can be assigned to all rings on the given specimen. The skeleton plot is only a summarizing device, and to be infernally sure of a tree-ring date, one must always return to the wood specimens for dating verification.

The history of the crossdating principle is interesting, for at least three scholars independently arrived at a similar, if unnamed, principle in the eighteenth and nineteenth centuries. In 1783, F.A.L. von Burgsdorf (1783) compared growth rings in several trees and several species and otherwise fulfilled all aspects of crossdating (see Studhalter 1955: 55), though he did not apply his technique to archaeological or historic structures in Germany. Half a century later, Alfred Twining (1833) crossdated several trees but again did not recognize the chronometric implications for archaeology. He wrote: "While inspecting and measuring that timber [in 1827] . . . I took particular notice of the successive layers, each of which constitutes a year of growth. These layers were of various breadth, indicating a growth five or six times as full in some years as in others. Thus, every tree had preserved a record of the seasons, for the whole period of its growth, whether 30 years or 200 and, what is worthy of observation, *every tree told the same story*" (Studhalter 1955: 56).

Charles Babbage, in an 1838 contribution titled "On the Age of Strata, as Inferred from the Rings of Trees Embedded in Them" (Babbage 1838; see Heizer 1962), made similar observations and developed a system for recording ring-widths based on their size and relationship to surrounding rings. Similar to Douglass's skeleton plot, the Babbage system used *o* to designate an ordinary ring, an *L* to denote a large ring, and an *s* for small rings, such that a ring sequence might look like this:

oLLosLssLLLLoLoossL . . .

Though Babbage improved on previous work by developing a recording system, he, like von Burgsdorf (1783) and Twining (1833), was not interested in developing a dating technique and certainly was not interested in archaeology. "Archaeologists," if they could be labeled as such, working at that time were also not interested in matters chronological, so these developments fell onto deaf ears. What, then, was different about Douglass's work in the second decade of the twentieth century? As we shall see, the difference was Clark Wissler of the American Museum of Natural History.

By training an astronomer, Douglass first became interested in the study of tree rings in 1901 while working at the Lowell Observatory in Flagstaff, Arizona (Bannister 1963; Douglass 1937; Glock 1933; Webb 1983). He realized that his research on sunspots would be greatly enhanced if he could find a long-term, terrestrial, proxy record of their activity, and he began looking for possible record sources. Given that tree growth was known to be partially dependent on rates of photosynthesis and therefore sunlight intensity, Douglass began examining stumps of long-lived coniferous trees left by loggers in the area.

Douglass first noted the possibilities of crossdating while inspecting tree stumps in Flagstaff in 1904, when he deduced, through rudimentary tree-ring analysis, that a particular tree in the area had been cut in 1894 (Towner 2000: 169). His deduction was confirmed by oral history: the local landowner admitted that he had in fact cut the tree ten years earlier. The full analytical implications of crossdating were not realized until 1911, however, when Douglass recognized the Flagstaff pattern of tree rings in trees from Prescott, Arizona, some 75 miles to the southwest. The geographic extent of the crossdating surprised Douglass and must have stirred him to action, for the period 1911 to 1920 is marked by intensified tree-ring analysis in his search for sunspot cycles. In 1914, Clark Wissler read one of Douglass's articles (1914) and recognized the chronometric possibilities in this technique, for Wissler was well aware that prehistoric wood beams were well preserved in cliff dwellings and other sites in Arizona and New Mexico.

If one accepts the commonsense notion that tree growth, like annual plant growth, starts and stops with the seasons, it does not take a very long inferential leap to realize that a count of the rings on a tree stump *might* indicate how old a tree was when it was cut. Many young children are kept occupied on camping trips by determining whether a particular pine tree is as old as their grandmother or grandfather. Unfortunately, things in nature are rarely so neat. Given the vagaries of weather, climate, competition, injury, infestation and a host of other variables, tree species that are otherwise appropriate for tree-ring dating might sometimes grow two rings in a season, no rings in a season, or a ring might be present on some portion of the stem but not on others. It is for this reason that ring counting by archaeologists or natural scientists cannot be considered dendrochronology.

Renaissance scholar Leonardo da Vinci apparently counted rings on stumps to infer age and climatic conditions, as did George Jean Louis Leclerc, Comte de Buffon (du Hamel and de Buffon 1737; see Studhalter 1955), Thomas Jefferson (1787), E. D. Cope (1879; see Fowler 2000), Jesse Walter Fewkes (1915), Jacob Kuechler (1859; see Studhalter 1955), and many others at various points in their scientific careers. Given that dendrochronology requires more than just ring counting, and that none of these scholars produced a master tree-ring chronology with which to compare their ring series, they were not doing tree-ring dating in a strict sense.

Jesse Walter Fewkes of the Smithsonian Institution's Bureau of American Ethnology counted 360 rings in a cedar (juniper) tree growing in the middle of Sun Temple at Mesa Verde National Park (Fewkes 1915). On that basis he argued that the tree, and therefore the structure, was at least 360 years old. This ring-counting effort likewise cannot be considered "dendrochronology," however, because it did not acknowledge the possibility that missing, locally absent, or double rings were present on the specimen in question (see Stokes and Smiley 1968). In addition, even if Fewkes had addressed these dendrochronological issues, a date from a tree growing on a site merely provides a date before which the site must have been occupied (a *terminus ante quem*) and is, therefore, of extremely limited analytic utility.

On June 15, 1935, archaeologist Warren K. Moorehead sent Douglass a reprint of his article in *Science* titled "A Forgotten Tree-Ring Record" (Moorehead 1934). In it he argued that he performed the first tree-ring dating of an archaeological site in North America when he counted rings on a walnut stump in the Midwest (see Moorehead 1890).

Fewkes and Moorehead are the only archaeologists in the above litany of ring counters. If archaeologists were so interested in chronology and temporal relationships around the turn of the century, and especially before 1914 (Lyman et al. 1997), why did not more of them, especially in the American Southwest, make the inferential leap from the commonsense notion that rings can be used to determine the age of a tree to the notion that ring-series preserved in archaeological beams might be used to determine the age of a site? I maintain that it is because archaeologists, as social rather than natural scientists, were not terribly interested in chronology of any kind. In addition, when they were interested in measuring time, as in the ring-counting efforts mentioned above, they were interested in categorical (for example, annual) dates, not in the tree-ring patterns from which they were derived in the Douglass system. It was Douglass (1929) who pointed out the paleoenvironmental potential of the ring series when he first used the term "Great Drought" to refer to the cause of the narrow and erratic tree-ring series of A.D. 1276–1299 on the Colorado Plateau.

A common factor in the development of chronological studies in general and tree-ring dating in particular in North America is Clark Wissler, who, with nearly every early mention of chronology in the literature, and in a fashion vaguely reminiscent of the "Where's Waldo?" puzzles, pops up somewhere in the archives. If you read of early attempts at archaeological chronology development, ask yourself, "Where's Wissler"? The interesting thing is that Wissler was not an archaeologist either; he was an anthropologist with training in psychology and became interested in dating to bolster his theories on culture areas and age areas. Nevertheless, Wissler, along with American Museum of Natural History colleagues Nelson, Spier, Kroeber, and Morris, and Kidder of the Peabody Museum at Phillips Academy, were busy developing a "new archaeology," of which chronology development and dating were critical components (see Fowler 2000: 275–293; Nash 1999: 19–35; Snead 2001: 97–125).

Clark Wissler

In 1909, during the time that Douglass was formulating his principle of crossdating, Wissler organized the Archer M. Huntington Survey of the Southwest for the American Museum of Natural History (Wissler 1919; see Fowler 2000; Snead 2001). An explicit goal of the survey was to discover the chronological relationships of the prehistoric ruins of the Southwest, and it was Wissler who first recognized the archaeological implications of Douglass's research (Wissler 1921). The first documented contact between the two is a letter from Wissler to Douglass dated May 22, 1914. Wissler had become interested in Douglass's work after reading "A Method for Estimating Rainfall by the Growth of Trees" (Douglass 1914). The 15-year effort to apply the Douglass method of tree-ring analysis to archaeological specimens began tentatively, if not in earnest, when Wissler wrote that day: "Your work suggests to me a possible help in the archaeological investigation of the Southwest." He expanded on this thought: "We do not know how old these ruins are, but I should be glad to have an opinion from you as to whether it might be possible to connect up with your modern and dated series of tree specimens [with wood specimens] from these [prehistoric] ruins by correlating the curves of growth. . . . I shall be glad to hear from you as to whether you think it is possible for us to secure any chronological data from the examination of this material."

As a result of this post, Pliny Earle Goddard, curator of ethnology at AMNH, assured Douglass, in a letter dated June 19, 1914, that "as soon as Mr. Nelson, one of our field men, reaches the Southwest he will be able to secure [for] you carefully identified material."[1] Goddard referred to Nels Nelson, who at the time was applying and refining stratigraphic excavation techniques in the Galisteo Basin of north-central New Mexico (Nelson 1914, 1916). Despite Goddard's assurances, there is only circumstantial evidence that Nelson ever submitted wood samples to Douglass for dating. A letter (November 6, 1934) from Douglass to H. F. Osborn of the American Museum suggests that Wissler and Nelson submitted tree-ring samples from Grand Gulch, Utah, but that the samples were complacent in their ring series and therefore useless for dating purposes. Nevertheless, it is curious that Nelson, who worked closely with Earl Morris, who by Nelson's own admission was an ardent tree-ring specimen collector (Nelson 1917), and whose own research and publications document a significant interest in chronology and chronological analysis (Nelson 1914, 1916), did not participate more fully in archaeological tree-ring research.

The first archaeological tree-ring samples analyzed by Douglass were collected in 1915 by a joint expedition of the AMNH and the University of Colorado in the Gobernador area of northwestern New Mexico. The specimens were apparently submitted to Douglass on March 21, 1916, but no record of the samples currently exists at the Laboratory of Tree-Ring Research at the University of Arizona. It is likely that Douglass did not have a curatorial system in place when the first specimens were submitted, and they may have been lost or destroyed.

In late April 1918, Wissler suggested to Douglass the intriguing possibility of using tree rings to date sites relatively, even if they could not yet be absolutely dated: "The point that appeals to me now is the possibility of comparing the timbers from the ruins in the Chaco Valley with those in the vicinity of Aztec. . . . I infer from your past work [that] it would be possible to determine whether those were contemporaneous or not. In any case, we shall try to furnish you with sections from timbers in both ruins together with parallel cuttings from living trees in the vicinity."[2] Douglass replied that such an analysis would be possible as long as the tree-ring sequence in specimens from each site had at least one 50-year segment in common, 50 rings being the minimum number sufficient to establish good crossdating.[3] Today, dendrochronologists prefer 100 or more rings at a minimum, though the actual number needed depends on the sensitivity of the climate signal recorded in any given specimen (see Stokes and Smiley 1968).

There is no correspondence between Wissler and Douglass from April 1918 to May 1919, but during that time Morris, as directed by Wissler, collected specimens from Aztec Ruin near Farmington, New Mexico, and Pueblo Bonito in Chaco Canyon, New Mexico. Morris dutifully submitted six samples from the former and three from the latter (Douglass 1921). On May 22, 1919, five years to the day after Wissler first approached Douglass, the latter reported to Wissler that he could prove, through crossdating, that the six samples from Aztec Ruin were cut within a period of two years. The specimens from Pueblo Bonito seemed not so satisfactory, but Douglass recognized, with no small degree of caution, a "fair possibility that (Pueblo Bonito) might have been built about 25 years before the Aztec Ruin, but I would not like to be quoted that the two were coexistent to that extent." Wissler's reply came by airmail less than one week later: "I have read this with a great deal of interest and congratulate you upon the progress made. I am now sure that you will be able to make a very important contribution to the archaeology of the Southwest" (May 28, 1919). In retrospect, Wissler's measured tone belies what must have been unbridled enthusiasm for Douglass's seminal accomplishment, especially given the published goals of the Archer M. Huntington Expedition. Douglass had, for the first time, calibrated the temporal relationship of two prehistoric sites against an annual, if not yet Christian, calendar.

The importance of Douglass's feat from a dendrochronological perspective cannot be overstated, for he had established crossdating in archaeological specimens, thus satisfying one of the conditions for successful dating. From an archaeological perspective, it is good to remember that two years later, at the Pueblo Bonito conference of 1921, there was still "among anthropologists in general a considerable indifference and even hostility to" the proposal for detailed considerations of chronology (letter Wissler to Sylvanus Morley, Aug 16, 1921). If this indifference was characteristic of archaeologists in general, then Wissler's perspective was clearly ahead of its time.

By the end of January 1920, Douglass had become more confident in the crossdating found in the nine specimens from Aztec and Pueblo Bonito: "A convincing cross-identification between Aztec and Puebla [sic] Bonito shows that the latter was built some 40 to 45 years before the former. . . . The relative dating of these ruins is now an accomplished fact and similar relative dating can probably be extended to many other ruins" (January 29, 1920).

The successes of 1919 led to a year of stocktaking, analysis, and the preparation of publications. Wissler continued to advocate sample collection by archaeologists in the field, though only one of the six major excavations in the field in 1920 cooperated. Kidder was at Pecos for the Phillips Academy of Andover, Massachusetts, Frederick Hodge was at Hawikuh for the Museum of the American Indian, Samuel Guernsey was in Tsegi Canyon for the Peabody Museum, Hewett was at Chetro Ketl for the School of American Research, and Fewkes was at Mesa Verde National Park for the Smithsonian Institution. None of these archaeologists submitted tree-ring samples to Douglass. Only Byron Cummings, working in Tsegi Canyon for the University of Arizona, submitted samples, and these may well have been collected by John Wetherill, not Cummings after all (Dean 1969: 103). It is not clear why the others did not submit tree-ring specimens, though ignorance of Douglass's work is certainly possible, for publication of this early archaeological tree-ring research did not occur until the following year (Douglass 1921; Wissler 1921). On the other hand, this small cohort of established professionals certainly knew each other and their research, and Wissler probably spoke with at least some of them about Douglass's research. Chronology was simply not a focus of their research.

Despite his own low priority for archaeological tree-ring research and the apparent lack of cooperation from eminent southwestern archaeologists, Douglass did not stop thinking about archaeological problems. By 1920 he had outlined a program of research that included the plans for a "beam expedition" of the sort that actually occurred later in the decade. In a letter to Wissler (May 27, 1920), Douglass argued for "a young archaeologist from some large institution with summer's time and . . . a Ford who will visit all possible ruins and take samples from all possible beams, especially those that are in place[,] with sketches and other data showing location of beam and other general facts regarding the ruin." The letter from which this passage was taken was, for reasons that remain unclear, never sent; the original remains on file at the University of Arizona Main Library Special Collections. The American Museum of Natural History's support of Douglass's tree-ring work through the Archer M. Huntington Expedition ended in 1920. The results of Douglass's and Wissler's research were subsequently published in *Natural History* in 1921 (Douglass 1921; Wissler 1921). Douglass's (1921) article was based on a paper he gave to anthropologists in Section H of the American Association for the Advancement of Science meetings in Chicago in late 1920 that presented, for the first time, his dendrochronological evidence for the relative dating of Aztec Ruin and Pueblo Bonito. Wissler's (1921) paper summarized the work of the Archer M. Huntington Survey as a whole, and he wrote triumphantly that tree-ring dating "is another improvement in our methods for dating ruins in the Southwest, and was first applied . . . by the Archer M. Huntington Survey" (Wissler 1921: 23). This reiteration is important because, in later publications, Neil Judd failed to properly credit the American Museum for its support of early archaeological tree-ring dating (Judd 1930, 1962, 1964, 1968).

In an effort to continue Douglass's archaeological tree-ring research, Wissler suggested that Judd, who at the time was planning long-term excavations at Pueblo Bonito for the National Geographic Society, contact Douglass to inquire about supporting long-term tree-ring research. Wissler made it clear to Judd that he regarded this work "as of very great importance since, by it, it is possible to determine the approximate time taken for the construction of the building and the relative ages of the different parts. It will also be possible, from chance finds of logs in the sediment nearby, to determine the time relation of the pueblo to these deposits" (March 26, 1921). Note that Wissler, and therefore Douglass, understood that crossdated tree-ring series could be used to establish prehistoric construction sequences as well as to date sites relatively, even if absolute dates could not yet be determined. Judd immediately replied that he would contact Douglass and learn the appropriate methods of sample recovery (March 26, 1921). On April 1, 1921, Judd wrote to Douglass and invited him to visit the Pueblo Bonito camp at Chaco Canyon. Douglass, however, knew nothing about young Judd, and lamented to Hewett on May 20, 1921, "I have had a letter of invitation from Mr. Judd. I have no idea how he happened to send it."

It is clear that Clark Wissler and the American Museum of Natural History were the archaeological forces that initiated the development of archaeological tree-ring dating. Wissler initially contacted Douglass in 1914, Morris collected the first archaeological tree-ring samples while he was employed by AMNH, and the American Museum funded Douglass's analyses through 1920. It is worth emphasizing that Douglass's (1921) and Wissler's (1921) articles established in print the American Museum's priority in tree-ring dating.

For all the lip service archaeologists pay to an interest in chronology and time, it is astonishing to me that more archaeologists did not become active in attempts to develop tree-ring dating prior to the National Geographic Society's support of Douglass's work. The reasons for this lack of interest are many, varied, and complex, yet almost certainly have to do with fundamental differences in analytical approaches to basic data in the social and natural sciences in general and archaeology and astronomy in particular. In short, archaeologists of that era were interested in identifying and describing types of objects. For them, the type was real and the variation was noise. Douglass, on the other hand, was interested in patterned variability in tree rings as a potential terrestrial record of sunspot variability. For him, the variability was real, while the type ("tree ring") was an abstraction.

Wissler was the only anthropologist realistically talking about "dating" our ruins at that time, and he was not an archaeologist. Nelson, one of the supposed pioneers in archaeological chronology, apparently did not actively support tree-ring dating, even though his boss recognized its research potential. It seems clear that archaeologists were not very interested in measuring time prior to 1921 in the American Southwest.

Notes

1. Goddard to Douglass, June 19, 1914. On file at the University of Arizona Special Collections, Douglass Papers, Box 68, Folder 2.
2. Wissler to Douglass, April 20, 1918, ibid.
3. Douglass to Wissler, April 30, 1918, ibid.

References

Babbage, C. 1838. "On the Age of Strata, as Inferred from the Rings of Trees Embedded in Them." Note M from *The Ninth Bridgewater Treatise* (cited in Heizer 1962).

Baillie, M.G.L. 1995. *A Slice Through Time: Dendrochronology and Precision Dating.* London: B. T. Batsford.

Baldwin, G. C. 1938. "Basketmaker and Pueblo Sandals." *Southwestern Lore* 4 (1): 1–6.

Bannister, B. 1963. "Dendrochronology." In *Science in Archaeology,* edited by D. Brothwell and E. Higgs, 162–176. London: Thames and Hudson.

Bannister, B., and W. J. Robinson. 1986. "Archaeology and Dendrochronology." In *Emil W. Haury's Prehistory of the American Southwest,* edited by J. J. Reid and D. E. Doyel, 49–54. Tucson: University of Arizona Press.

Browman, D. L., and D. R. Givens. 1996. "Stratigraphic Excavation: The First 'New Archaeology.'" *American Anthropologist* 98 (1): 80–95.

Burgsdorf, F.A.L. von. 1783. *Versuch einer vollständigen Geschichte vorzüglicher Holzarten, etc.* [Attempting a complete history of superior woods.] Vol. 1.

Chazan, M. 1996. "Conceptions of Time and the Development of Paleolithic Chronology." *American Anthropologist* 97 (3): 457–467.

Cole, F.-C. 1934. *Dendrochronology in the Mississippi Valley.* Committee on State Archaeological Surveys, Division of Anthropology and Psychology, National Research Council, Circular Series no. 16.

Cope, E. D. 1879. "Report on the Remains of Population Observed in Northwestern New Mexico." In *Archaeology,* edited by F. W. Putnam, 351–361, vol. 7, *Report upon Geographical and Geological Explorations and Surveys West of the One Hundredth Meridian, in charge of Lt. George M. Wheeler, Corps of Engineers.* Washington, D.C.: Government Printing Office.

Cornelius, O. F. 1938. "Basketmaker Sandals (?)." *Southwestern Lore* 3 (4): 74–78.

Daniel, G. 1963. *The Idea of Prehistory.* Cleveland: World Publishing.

Dark, K. R. 1995. *Theoretical Archaeology.* London: Duckworth.

Dean, J. S. 1969. *Chronological Analysis of Tsegi Phase Sites in Northeastern Arizona.* Papers of the Laboratory of Tree-Ring Research, no. 3. University of Arizona, Tucson.

———. 1978. "Independent Dating in Archaeological Analysis." In *Advances in*

Archaeological Method and Theory, edited by M. B. Schiffer, 1:223–265. New York: Academic Press.

Dixon, R. B. 1913. "Some Aspects of North American Archaeology." *American Anthropologist* 15 (4): 549–573.

Douglass, A. E. 1914. "A Method for Estimating Rainfall by the Growth of Trees." *Carnegie Institution of Washington Publication* 192:101–121.

———. 1921. "Dating our Prehistoric Ruins: How Growth Rings in Timbers Aid in Establishing the Relative Ages of the Ruined Pueblos of the Southwest." *Natural History* 21 (2): 27–30.

———. 1929. "The Secret of the Southwest Solved by Talkative Tree-Rings." *National Geographic* 56 (6): 736–770.

———. 1937. *Tree-Rings and Chronology*. University of Arizona Bulletin 8 (4); Physical Sciences Bulletin 1. Tucson.

———. 1941. "Crossdating in Dendrochronology." *Journal of Forestry* 39 (10): 825–831.

Du Hamel, M., and G. J. L. Leclerc, Compte de Buffon. 1737. "Observations Des Différents Effects Que Produisent Sur Les Vegétaux, Les Grandes Gelées D'hiver & Les Petites Gelées Du Printemps" [Of the various effects on vegetation of the large frosts of winter and the small frosts of spring]. *Memoires de l'Academie Royale des Sciences de Paris* 1737:273–298.

Fewkes, J. W. 1915. "A Sun Temple in Mesa Verde National Park." *Art and Archaeology* 2:341–346.

Fowler, D. D. 2000. *A Laboratory for Anthropology: Science and Romanticism in the American Southwest, 1846–1930*. Albuquerque: University of New Mexico Press.

Fritts, H. C. 1976. *Tree-Rings and Climate*. New York: Academic Press.

Glock, W. S. 1933. "Tree-Ring Analysis on Douglass System." *Pan-American Geologist* 60: 1–14.

Haury, E. W. 1930. "A Study of Pinyon with Respect to Its Possible Use as a Dating Wood." Unpublished manuscript on file at the Laboratory of Tree-Ring Research, University of Arizona.

———. 1934. *The Canyon Creek Ruin and the Cliff Dwellings of the Sierra Ancha*. Medallion Papers 14. Gila Pueblo, Globe, Ariz.

———. 1935. "Tree-Rings: The Archaeologist's Time Piece." *American Antiquity* 1 (2): 98–108.

———. 1946. "Tree Rings and Archaeology." Unpublished manuscript on file at Arizona State Museum Archives, Box 94–120.

———. 1995. "Wherefore a Harvard Ph.D.?" *Journal of the Southwest* 37 (4): 710–717.

Heizer, R. F. 1962. *Man's Discovery of His Past: Literary Landmarks in Archaeology*. Englewood Cliffs, N.J.: Prentice-Hall.

Hewett, E. L. 1930. *Ancient Life in the Southwest*. Indianapolis: Bobbs-Merrill.

Jefferson, T. 1787. *Notes on the State of Virginia.* London: John Stockdale. Reprint, Chapel Hill: University of North Carolina Press, 1954.

Judd, N. M. 1930. "Dating Our Prehistoric Pueblo Ruins." In *Explorations and Fieldwork of the Smithsonian Institution in 1929,* 167–176. Washington: Smithsonian Institution.

———. 1962. "Andrew Ellicott Douglass, 1867–1962." *American Antiquity* 28: 87–89.

———. 1964. *The Architecture of Pueblo Bonito.* Smithsonian Miscellaneous Collections 147 (1).

———. 1968. *Men Met along the Trail: Adventures in Archaeology.* Norman: University of Oklahoma Press.

Kidder, A. V. 1924. *An Introduction to the Study of Southwestern Archaeology.* Andover, Mass.: Phillips Academy.

———. 1927. "The Museum's Expedition to Canon de Chelly and Canyon del Muerto, Arizona." *Natural History* 27 (3): 203–209.

———. 1936. "Speculations on New World Prehistory." In *Essays in Anthropology Presented to A. L. Kroeber in Celebration of His Sixtieth Birthday, June 11, 1936,* edited by R. H. Lowie, 143–152. Berkeley and Los Angeles: University of California Press.

———. 1958. *Pecos, New Mexico: Archaeological Notes.* Papers of the Robert S. Peabody Foundation for Archaeology, no. 5. Andover, Mass.

Kroeber, A. 1916. "Zuni Culture Sequences." *Proceedings of the National Academy of Sciences* 2: 42–45.

Kuechler, J. 1859. "Das Klima von Texas" [The climate of Texas]. *Texas Staats-Zeitung,* August 6, 1859. San Antonio, Texas.

Laufer, B. 1913. "Remarks on 'Some Aspects of North American Archaeology.'" *American Anthropologist* 15 (4): 573–577.

Lyman, R. L., M. J. O'Brien, and R. C. Dunnell. 1997. *The Rise and Fall of Culture History.* New York: Plenum.

McElvaine, R. S. 1993. *The Great Depression: America, 1929–1941.* New York: Times Books.

Meltzer, D. J. 1985. "North American Archaeology and Archaeologists: 1879–1934." *American Antiquity* 50 (2): 241–260.

Moorehead, W. K. 1890. *Fort Ancient: The Great Prehistoric Earthwork of Warren County, Ohio.* Cincinnati: R. Clarke.

———. 1934. "A Forgotten Tree-Ring Record." *Science* 80 (2062): 16–17.

Nash, S. E. 1999. *Time, Trees, and Prehistory: Tree-Ring Dating and the Development of North American Archaeology, 1914–1950.* Salt Lake City: University of Utah Press.

Nash, S., and J. S. Dean. In press. "Paleoenvironmental Reconstructions and Archaeology: Uniting the Social and Natural Sciences in the American Southwest and Beyond." In *One Hundred Years of Southwestern Archaeology: The Transformation of a Discipline,* edited by D. Fowler and L. Cordell. Tucson: University of Arizona Press.

Nelson, N. C. 1914. *Pueblo Ruins of the Galisteo Basin, New Mexico.* American Museum of Natural History, Anthropological Papers 15 (1): 1–124.

———. 1916. "Chronology of the Tano Ruins, New Mexico." *American Anthropologist* 18 (2): 159–180.

———. 1917. "Excavation of Aztec Ruin." *American Museum Journal* 17 (2): 85–99.

———. 1918. "Chronology in Florida." *American Museum of Natural History, Anthropological Papers* 22 (2): 75–103.

Renaud, E. 1928. "Evolution of Population and Dwellings in the Indian Southwest." *El Palacio* 26 (5): 75–86.

Roberts, F.H.H. 1935. "A Summary of Southwestern Archaeology." *American Anthropologist* 37 (1): 1–35.

———. 1937. "Archaeology in the Southwest." *American Antiquity* 3 (1): 3–33.

Shanks, M., and C. Tilley. 1987. *Social Theory and Archaeology.* Albuquerque: University of New Mexico Press.

Snead, J. E. 2001. *Ruins and Rivals: The Making of Southwest Archaeology.* Tucson: University of Arizona Press.

Spier, L. 1917a. "Zuni Chronology." *Proceedings of the National Academy of Sciences* 3: 280–283.

———. 1917b. "An Outline for a Chronology of Zuni Ruins." *American Museum of Natural History, Anthropological Papers* 18 (3): 207–331.

———. 1931. "N. C. Nelson's Stratigraphic Technique in the Reconstruction of Prehistoric Sequences in Southwestern America." In *Methods in Social Science: A Case Book,* edited by Stuart A. Rice, 275–283. Chicago: University of Chicago Press.

Stokes, M. A., and T. L. Smiley. 1968. *An Introduction to Tree-Ring Dating.* Chicago: University of Chicago Press.

Studhalter, R. A. 1955. "Tree Growth: Some Historical Chapters." *Botanical Review* 21 (1–3): 1–72.

Towner, R. H. 2000. "Concordance and Discordance in Navajo Archaeology." In *It's About Time: A History of Archaeological Dating in North America,* edited by S. E. Nash, 168–185. Salt Lake City: University of Utah Press.

Twining, A. C. 1833. "On the Growth of Timber." *American Journal of Scientific Arts* 24: 391–393.

Webb, G. S. 1983. *Tree-Rings and Telescopes.* Tucson: University of Arizona Press.

Willey, G. R., and J. A. Sabloff. 1980. *A History of American Archaeology.* 2d ed. San Francisco: W. H. Freeman.

Wissler, C. 1919. "The Archer M. Huntington Survey of the Southwest, Zuni District." *American Museum of Natural History, Anthropological Papers* 18: i–ix.

———. 1921. "Dating Our Prehistoric Ruins." *Natural History* 21 (1): 13–26.

Zeuner, F. E. 1951. *Dating the Past: An Introduction to Geochronology.* New York: Longmans, Green.

Contributors

David L. Browman is a professor of anthropology at Washington University in St. Louis.

Andrew L. Christenson is an independent scholar living in Prescott, Arizona.

Robert C. Dunnell is professor emeritus in anthropology at the University of Washington and is affiliated with Mississippi State University, the University of Tennessee, and the Yale Peabody Museum.

Stephen E. Nash is head of collections in anthropology at the Field Museum in Chicago.

Michael J. O'Brien is professor of anthropology and associate dean in the College of Arts and Science at the University of Missouri–Columbia.

James E. Snead is assistant professor of anthropology at George Mason University in Fairfax, Virginia.

James Truncer is a lecturer on anthropological sciences at Stanford University and a research associate with the California Academy of Sciences.

Index